Fear and Faith will serve to provide much needed encouragement to many women who may think they are the only ones suffering through crises. Trillia's candid personal testimony coupled with real-life stories from other women all testify that none is beyond the reach of Christ's redeeming love toward us. —MARY K. MOHLER, director, Seminary Wives Institute of The Southern Baptist Theological Seminary

I'm so happy that Trillia wrote this book. It offers real hope for women who are burdened and burned out by the fears that confront them on a daily basis. *Fear and Faith* offers a wonderful reminder that we don't have to "perform" any longer, because our loving God cherishes and accepts us just as we are. —KELLY ROSATI, vice president of community outreach, Focus on the Family

Trillia's writing style is her winsome honesty. In *Fear and Faith*, she bares her heart and allows us to walk close beside her in a personal journey with fear. Thank you, Trillia, for not only challenging those of us who struggle with fear, but also for clearly leading us on the pathway to true peace! —KIMBERLY WAGNER, author, *Fierce Women*

We can all identify with the destructive and paralyzing results of living by fear. As Christians we long for lives defined instead by faith and God's power. Trillia reminds us why we can trust God and holds out a vision for life defined by this kind of trust—fearing God rather than our feelings, fears, and fellow travelers. —AMY SIMPSON, author, *Anxious: Choosing Faith in a World of Worry*

Trillia Newbell, one of the most joy-filled people I know, bares her struggles with fear and the well-worn path she's found to faith. As a chronic fearer, I was much encouraged by *Fear and Faith*. —LORE FERGUSON, writer, thinker, and tinkerer at sayable.net

Fear has been a companion much of my life, robbing me of much joy. In *Fear and Faith*, Trillia gently and compassionately explores fears common to many women and points fearful hearts to the One who has set us free from all fear. —CHRISTINA FOX, licensed mental health counselor, writer, blogger: toshowthemjesus.com

When fear and anxiety hit like a tidal wave, trusting God isn't always easy. Trillia's message is that fear doesn't have to pin us to the mat. In a style that is helpful, conversational, and deeply rooted in God's Word, Trillia gives real, meaningful hope to the fearful. Every woman needs this book! —ERIN DAVIS, author, speaker, blogger

Praise for *Fear and Faith*

Trillia serves us well in this book by addressing fear and anxiety head-on and digs past the fear itself and into the very roots where fear is born. She does this with the gentleness of a mother and a mind steeped in the Bible. Whether you personally struggle with fear or walk with people who do, you will find helpful, well thought-out help in the pages of this book.
—MATT CHANDLER, lead pastor, The Village Church, Dallas, Texas; author, *The Explicit Gospel*

Trillia Newbell knows what it is to be plagued by fear. She also knows what it is to fight for faith and to ground her heart in the character of our wise, faithful, loving, sovereign God. She offers hope for overcoming our fears and experiencing true peace, through cultivating reverential fear of the Lord.
—NANCY DEMOSS WOLGEMUTH, author; host of *Revive Our Hearts*

Many Christians are scared, and too scared to say that they are scared. Trillia Newbell helps us confront our fears and point beyond them to a Christ who has vanquished every foe. This book grapples with heavy subjects but with the joyful gravity of a woman anointed with the Spirit and with wisdom. —RUSSELL D. MOORE, president, Southern Baptist Ethics & Religious Liberty Commission

Trillia puts her finger on *the* thing that, for many of us, keeps our faith subdued and our lives joyless: fear. She writes with humility, authenticity, and victory. This book will bless you and release you. —J. D. GREEAR, author, *Jesus, Continued . . . Why the Spirit Inside You Is Better Than Jesus Beside You*

We love Trillia Newbell's insights into common fears, and her vulnerability and transparency about her own struggles. Trillia's heart is opened beautifully on these pages. *Fear and Faith* is a warm, honest, hope-giving, Christ-centered book that will deepen your trust in God. —RANDY AND NANCI ALCORN, authors of *Help for Women under Stress*

Trillia speaks from her heart and experience to all of us who find ourselves gripped by fear over what other people think, what might happen, or what might never happen, pointing us toward the freedom to be found in being gripped by a very different kind of fear—the fear of the Lord. —NANCY GUTHRIE, Bible teacher and author of *Hearing Jesus Speak into Your Sorrow*

It is refreshing to see such raw transparency as Trillia goes in depth with real-life stories and fears that we all struggle with as women. It is freeing to read biblical solutions of how to overcome those fears. I encourage women of all ages and walks of life to read this book. —NAGHMEH ABEDINI, wife of Pastor Saeed Abedini, who has been imprisoned in Iran for his Christian faith.

Though Trillia Newbell writes mainly with women in mind, she speaks to all of us disordered and disoriented fearers in this book. And she reminds us that the more the right fear governs us, the weaker our wrong fears become. *Fear and Faith* was a tonic to my soul. —JON BLOOM, president of Desiring God, author of *Not By Sight* and *Things Not Seen*.

Fears fester and grow in the darkness of the "what ifs." But oh! When the light shines! Trillia has good news for all of us who are tempted to live in fear. The what ifs have nowhere to hide from the brilliant "since God did not spare His own Son" of the gospel. Come bask in the light. —GLORIA FURMAN, author, *Glimpses of Grace, The Pastor's Wife*.

Trillia addresses real fears while drawing our attention upward to our very real God. He is good, sovereign, and lovingly able to address our individual fears as He calls us to personally trust Him. Being cemented in God's word is what our soul desperately needs since we are often drawn toward sinful fears rather than a healthy fear of God. —BLAIR LINNE, outspoken word artist, pastor's wife

If you've ever thought you were alone in your fears, and if you've ever told yourself that fear is not a problem for you, this book will challenge you to examine the truth of that statement. This grace-filled book will help you reclaim the energy given to fearfulness and redirect it toward faith in an infinitely trustworthy God. —JEN WILKIN, author, *Women of the Word*

This mind-calming, soul-pacifying book will transform many fear-full women into faith-full women. It will also help many men understand their wives better and therefore serve them more patiently, lovingly, and skillfully. —DAVID MURRAY, pastor, professor, author, *The Happy Christian*

In *Fear and Faith*, Trillia Newbell has given the church a valuable resource. With gentleness, humility, and boldness Trillia unfolds the pages of her life for us and then points us over and over again to Jesus, the author and perfecter of our faith. —JESSICA THOMPSON, author/speaker

Trillia Newbell digs deep down into our feminine hearts to expose the roots of our fears—roots of pride and unbelief and covetousness. And then she helps us face into those fears as she carefully applies the words of our faithful God who encourages us to "Fear not!" This book is full of wisdom and truth that you will want to return to time and again. —JANI ORTLUND, VP of Renewal Ministries, author, *His Loving Law*

FEAR AND FAITH

FINDING THE PEACE
YOUR HEART CRAVES

Trillia J. Newbell

MOODY PUBLISHERS

CHICAGO

All Scripture quotations, unless otherwise indicated, are taken from the Holy Bible, English Standard Version® (ESV®), copyright © 2001 by Crossway, a publishing ministry of Good News Publishers. Used by permission. All rights reserved.

Scripture quotations marked NIV are taken from the Holy Bible, New International Version®, NIV®. Copyright © 1973, 1978, 1984, 2011 by Biblica, Inc.™ Used by permission of Zondervan. All rights reserved worldwide. www.zondervan.com. The "NIV" and "New International Version" are trademarks registered in the United States Patent and Trademark Office by Biblica, Inc.™

All emphases in Scripture quotations have been added by the author.

Published in association with the literary agency Wolgemuth and Associates Inc.

Editor: Lydia Brownback
Interior Design: Ragont Design
Cover Design: Erik M. Peterson
Cover photos of open Bible copyright © 2014 by Brightside/Lightstock.
 of group of hands copyright © 2013 by Kerry Murphy/Stocksy.
 of hands with flower copyright © 2013 by Jacqueline Miller/Stocksy.
 of woman at beach copyright © 2014 by Jacqueline Miller/Stocksy.
 of woman window silhouette copyright © 2014 by Jacqueline Miller/Stocksy.
 of trees in fog copyright © 2014 by Jesse Weinberg/Stocksy.
 of woman holding mirror copyright © 2014 by Alexey Kuzma/Stocksy.
 of plane wing copyright © 2014 by Paul Edmondson/Stocksy.
 of child opening door copyright © 2014 by Saptak Ganguly/Stocksy.
All rights reserved on all of above photos.
Author Photo: Lillian Prince Photography

Library of Congress Cataloging-in-Publication Data

Newbell, Trillia J.
 Fear and faith : finding the peace your heart craves / Trillia J. Newbell.
  pages cm
 Includes bibliographical references.
 ISBN 978-0-8024-1022-1
 1. Fear—Religious aspects—Christianity. I. Title.
 BV4908.5.N49 2015
 248.4—dc23
                          2014044936

All websites and phone numbers listed herein are accurate at the time of publication, but may change in the future or cease to exist. The listing of website references and resources does not imply publisher endorsement of the site's entire contents. Groups and organizations are listed for informational purposes, and listing does not imply publisher endorsement of their activities.

We hope you enjoy this book from Moody Publishers. Our goal is to provide high-quality, thought-provoking books and products that connect truth to your real needs and challenges. For more information on other books and products written and produced from a biblical perspective, go to www.moodypublishers.com or write to:

Moody Publishers
820 N. LaSalle Boulevard
Chicago, IL 60610

5 7 9 10 8 6

Printed in the United States of America

To my husband, Thern, and our two children.
I thank God daily that I get to do life with you.
You are a joy, delight, and blessing to me! I love you!

CONTENTS

Preface	11
Introduction	13
1. Fear of Man	19
2. Fear of the Future	33
3. Fear of Other Women	41
4. Fear of Tragedy	51
5. Fear of Not Measuring Up	63
6. Fear of Physical Appearance	75
7. Fear of Sexual Intimacy	87
8. Why We Can Trust God	101
9. The Fear of the Lord	115
10. When Your Fears Come True	121
11. Growing in the Fear of the Lord	143
Appendix 1: Eating Disorders	153
Appendix 2: A Hedge of Doubt	165
Notes	169
Acknowledgments	173

PREFACE

F ear isn't just something that I'm somewhat familiar with; it's a temptation that has plagued me for as long as I can remember. As a young child, I was afraid of dogs, but as I've grown into adulthood, my fears have become more sophisticated and heart-wrenching. I've struggled with fears such as other people and the loss of a child. As I've spoken and interacted with women around the country, I realize I'm not alone. *Fear and Faith* is, in part, a book letting you know that you are not alone in your struggle with fear.

One of the special features of the book are the sections dedicated to telling the stories of other women, like you and me, who have battled fear. These women come from a broad range of life stages and backgrounds, but all have one thing in common: they've found the Lord to be faithful.

But it wouldn't be enough if we simply relied on the stories of others. In the pages ahead, you'll see most importantly that Jesus is also with you. He was tempted in every way, including the temptation to fear, but was without sin. Jesus relates to you and has comfort and peace stored up for you in His goodness and by His grace.

We will also explore who God is and why we can trust Him. How does God's sovereignty, goodness, love, and wisdom affect the way we respond to our temptations to fear? Can God truly be trusted? I'm praying that through these biblical truths and stories from others, this short book will help you find the peace your heart craves. I crave it too!

Like all books, this one has its limitations. If I were with you in flesh and blood, encouraging and counseling you through your current struggle, I might advise you to seek a counselor, a pastor, or other professional, depending on your situation. May I do that now? If you are presently in a place of deep pain and struggle, please, by all means, read this book! But don't stop there. Don't be ashamed to seek the help you need.

May these pages be a comfort to you.

Blessings,

Trillia

INTRODUCTION

R ight now, as I begin to type the pages of this book and ponder fear and the fear of the Lord, I'm riding on a plane with terrible (and terrifying) turbulence. We are bouncing up and down and being tossed from side to side. I have no control, no (reasonable) way out of this, and I'll be honest: I don't like it. I don't enjoy this feeling of helplessness, like my existence is in the hands of a stranger—who, I assume, has years of flying under his belt. But my anxious heart and mind begins to wonder, *What if he doesn't?* What if he panics and overcompensates, or what if this plane decides it no longer wants to work?

Those are the real thoughts swirling in my brain right this minute. And here I am, writing a book about fear and faith? This seems ridiculous. I'm terrified on a bumpy plane ride, and statistically I should be fine. But much greater than statistics that skew heavily in my favor is the fact that God is in control. Yet my fears continue. I'm writing as a woman who struggles with fears regularly and is fighting for faith. I am very much in the process of learning what it means to fear the Lord. I have not mastered the art of trusting the Lord. I'm learning, and, thankfully, God is patient with me. You might be like me: a Christian who firmly believes God is in control and yet still struggles with fear. Don't we all struggle with fear to one degree or another? God is patient with you too.

———— ✦ ————

I find Paul to be a wonderful example of a God-fearing man who had to learn to trust. He had to learn to be content (Philippians 4:11). Paul hadn't arrived. He was tried by fire. He was tested, and his faith and trust in the Lord grew as a result. I share this because you and I so often hold the men and women in Scripture as our example for life. The example from Paul is one of learning—not of perfection. The valiant woman of Proverbs is another example of a biblical character we may elevate. She laughed at the unknowns in the days to come and found her security and strength in the fear of the Lord (Proverbs 31:25, 30). She is the quintessential biblical example of a strong and courageous woman. When I envision her, I imagine she is unruffled by uncertainty and ready to face any danger.

Boy, do I wish I were like her! Thankfully, that is why she is considered an *ideal*. I, however, would characterize my everyday walk with the Lord quite differently. I am fearful, but I want to be bold and trusting. I am anxious, but I want to find confidence and rest in God. I imagine that the valiant woman, if walking the earth, wouldn't be comfortable with the pedestal we've put her on. No one is perfect, and even the "ideal" woman needed to grow and learn.

Similarly, you and I are tried. We don't become Christians and suddenly understand what it means to walk by faith. Like a baby, we may begin our journey by pushing off from our hands, then crawling, pulling up on the Word of truth, and failing and falling many times. And then one day we reach the point where we take that sure step of faith, and before we know it, we are wobbling toward a straight path. We aren't born walking from our mother's womb, and we aren't born again trusting perfectly.

I'm not alone in this. Just the other day I received an email from a friend, requesting prayer because she was afraid to leave her daughter as she traveled across the state. Before that, and over the past several months, I've had the privilege of caring for women who have had miscarriages, and they fear having more or never getting pregnant again. I have a dear college-aged friend who shared that she was afraid she might not do well enough on a midterm to pass her college class; and my single girlfriend is praying that the Lord will bring her a husband—but the prospect seems dim, so she fears it just won't happen. I could go on. And I imagine you resonate with similar temptations and circumstances.

We too often fear the past, the present, and the future. There is the fear of being who we are, so we try to please people. We, unlike the psalmist in Psalm 23, are afraid that the future is not as good as God says; *will goodness and mercy* really *follow me all my days?* (Psalm 23:6). There is the fear of other women, and—as a result—we compare ourselves to them and judge their actions and motives. We fear the future with anxious thoughts about our children not knowing the Lord when they get older or about our husband not returning from a trip. We don't want our kids to die, so we fixate on death and forget who is really in control. And we wonder if we are good enough for anyone or anything.

I know this to be true firsthand. From trusting God for a husband to praying that I wouldn't have another miscarriage, I've experienced the intense and debilitating temptation to fear. The fear I am referring to is by definition an expectation of harm; it is to be alarmed and apprehensive. When I am tempted to fear in this way, it is because my false sense of control has been altered by a circumstance. Or there are unknowns—what lies in the future—and I realize I have absolutely no control over what will happen. In many ways, our fears rest in seeking trust and security in ourselves. Within a matter of seconds I can bury my husband in my private thoughts; I've arranged the funeral and am now terrified as I try to figure out how to raise our two beautiful children by myself. These thoughts are imaginary; it hasn't happened. It's just my fear. During those times my mind isn't meditating on what is true, honorable, just, pure, lovely, commendable, excellent, and worthy of praise (Philippians 4:8). I've noticed that my decision to play God never works out well for me. Can you relate? Regardless, I think you and I do this because we believe it's easier to be in control. But when we realize we don't reign supreme, that we don't have sovereign authority over our lives, it can be terrifying.

There is, however, and thankfully, a remedy for all our fears. That remedy comes as a person, and the means through which He provides the comfort, along with the Holy Spirit, is through His Word. To fight our fears, we will look at God's sovereignty and love and watch our fears dissipate as we apply God's Word to our lives. The very thing we are holding on to (control) is, ironically, the thing we most need to let go of. As you and I come to understand that our God isn't ruling as a tyrant but is lovingly guiding and instructing as a Father, we can loosen the tight grip on our lives that produces the bad fruit of fear. This isn't "Let go and let God." It's "Let go, run hard toward your Savior, and learn to trust God."

There is, however, a fear that we want to possess. It is a fear defined as an awestruck wonder of the holy God who condescended to become a man, died on a cross, and bore the entire wrath that you and I deserve so that we might now enter into His presence. We can enter His presence and receive grace. He can turn our weak and sinful fear into a fear of Him. That's what He does; He turns coal into diamonds. We don't have to be crippled by fear, because we have a God who holds the oceans in the hollow of His hand. He doesn't promise that our lives will be easy (far from it), but He does promise to take care of us, His daughters, till the very end and for all of eternity. Ultimately we fight fear by trusting in the Lord and fearing Him.

Fear is an emotion we can feel in a variety of ways; it can be paralyzing, controlling, and even motivating. Unfortunately, fear is often a by-product of the sin in our heart. Fear has a way of whispering lies to our souls about who God is. But are there good forms of fear (aside from the fear of God described above)? Can it ever be legitimate or righteous, or is it always sinful? While assuredly the most acceptable fear is the fear of the Lord, there are times when fear is acceptable or even wise. In the chapters ahead, I'll dive into what constitutes an acceptable fear. And, to be clear, I'm not advocating reckless fearlessness. I'm not saying you should go find a cliff to jump off or that you need to build a bucket list filled with stunts and dares that, before reading this book, you'd never have done. That's not what I'm writing about. I'm writing about the fears we battle while living out our normal, everyday lives, which may or may not include cliff jumping.

So I ask you to crawl, wobble, and walk with me through the trials and fears we face as we learn to replace our fears with trust and to fear the Lord. We are given to fear, and we desire control, but the Lord has something better for us. The Lord has the better way—a way that will give us life and peace.

Fear and Faith is about how, when we place our security in the Lord, we too can wear strength as our clothing (Proverbs 31:17).

———◆———

The plane continues to wobble and bounce; oh, how I wish it wouldn't! But, as we descend and toss back and forth, I realize that I have a choice. Right now I'm faced with the choice of either gritting my teeth and imagining my kids' and husband's life without me or trusting the Lord. In this instance—and by God's grace—I choose to trust, and, in the pages ahead, I'll tell you about how I've come to a better (still much to learn!) place of trusting.

Chapter 1

FEAR OF MAN

When I first became a Christian, I remember feeling carefree, and to say I was excited about the Lord would have been an understatement. I was also a sponge. Anything anyone said to me about my newfound faith I took as "the gospel." As you might imagine, for a young, impressionable Christian this was not good. I didn't fully understand grace, and as people would talk about sin, I began to become fearful of not measuring up. I began to live in fear of sinning. I began to question my motives, actions, thoughts—everything—and assume everyone was questioning them too! I was afraid of the judgment of others. I was terrified of the opinions of others. I judged others in fear, and I feared man.

"Fear of man" is a term used to describe the heart of someone who acts or says, or does *not* act or say, certain things out of fear of what others may think. There's an example of it in Scripture, in John 12, when the people and authorities believed in Jesus but would not confess it for fear that they would be shunned (John 12:42–43). Even Peter, who walked with Christ and was one of His disciples, denied Him three times because of his fear of man (Mark 14:66–72). Caring deeply about what others think can be damaging to our faith and bring great despair. At least that was the case for me.

The Many Cares of What Others Think

Sin isn't a foreign concept. It is that unfortunate condition we face at birth and which remains in us until that moment when the Lord takes us home. I have sinned, I continue to sin, and I will sin more. But in my pride, there was a time when I didn't want anyone to think that I did sin. I hated the idea of disappointing anyone. It didn't come to light for me until I was a young-adult Christian, but it was something that I had battled all my life—pleasing people.

I was the all-star cheerleader, flute-playing band geek, honor student, student-government president, and good girl (except with boys—I liked boys at a young age). I was *that* girl. The overachiever, friends with everyone, always smiling (I was genuinely a happy girl and okay—some things haven't changed, but now it's the joy of the Lord), typical goody two-shoes. I had a secret though: I loved the praise of people and hated the idea of doing wrong. The most important person in my life as a young girl was my father, and I wanted most to please him.

So I worked hard, generally obeyed (we didn't have many rules), and excelled in extracurricular activities and school. I think this fear of man and desire to honor my father was actually a God-given, gracious wedge of protection. Kids were experimenting with drugs, and I didn't want anything to do with that. I wasn't a partier, but I did have a "serious" relation-ship as a young girl with a boy and remember talking about that carnal relationship with my father. It was my respect for him that led me to cut it off. There was a healthy respect and fear in that instance, which I'll write about later, but, overall, many of my actions were simply a desire to please and be seen as doing good. My father did instill in me a love for people, so not everything I did was to people please, but the idea of disappointing my father tore me up inside.

So when I became a Christian in my twenties, and the Holy Spirit began to reveal my sinful heart, I was astonished. I couldn't believe that there was a possibility that part of my motivation to do good and be all that I could be was actually born out of sin. After all, I was a good person, right? My pride was so great that I was condemned. Ultimately the problem with my people pleasing was that I had come to believe that the opinions of others about me were far greater than God's.

Lou Priolo wrote in his book *Pleasing People* that one of the many temptations a people pleaser might face is "an excessive love of praise [that] tempts you to believe man's opinion of yourself over God's opinion."[1] The foolishness of this temptation is that the men and women we seek to please are just like us—fallible.

This fear of man is manifested in many ways. In my life, it was all about looking good and, as I mentioned earlier, doing my best not to disappoint my father. (Ironically, it was terri-bly hard to disappoint my father. He was incredibly gracious, which is what made my fear that much sillier.) For others the fear might be driven by a desire to fit into a certain group or by a desire not to be associated with a certain person.

Perhaps you refuse to associate with certain people, rejecting them in order to appear a certain way to others. Social media has a way of pulling out the fear of man. We check to see who has "liked" our post or picture, fearing what we write, hoping to be noticed.

You've heard the saying, "There is nothing new under the sun" (Ecclesiastes 1:9). It's definitely true regarding the fear of man. Peter (you know, the man who received the keys to the kingdom) denied his friend and Savior not once but *three* times. He didn't deny Him during happy days. He denied Christ on the way to Christ's death, and he did it out of the fear of man. Looking into this account from Peter's life will give you and me a glimpse into the motivations and consequences of this fear.

Jesus had prophesied that Peter would deny Him, but Peter strongly objected, saying, "If I must die with you, I will not deny you" (Mark 14:31). He fell into the trap of believing that he was above this sin. Paul warns us that if we think we stand, we must "take heed lest [we] fall" (1 Corinthians 10:12). No one is completely immune to certain temptations, but Peter was sure of himself. He was sure that he would stand strong with Jesus, facing the authorities and mockers, till the bitter end (Mark 14:29).

You know, however, how it turns out. Peter did not stand with Christ and denied Him twice to a servant girl and then to an entire crowd. Peter knew immediately after that rooster crowed that he had failed the test that he'd been sure he was going to pass. Peter didn't continue in pride or make excuses for his denial. He fell to the ground and wept. I imagine the tears were many. He had betrayed his friend, teacher, and Savior for fear of his own life being taken from him. Peter didn't want to die. At that moment Peter forgot what it meant to follow Christ.

When we fear man, we join Peter in his moment of forgetfulness. Peter forgot that those who kill the body cannot kill the soul (Matthew 10:28). You will see that Scripture passage referenced in various ways throughout this book because it is packed, in just a few short words, with an ocean of theological truth about the fear of the Lord. There is only one whom we need to fear, and that is the Lord. But Peter forgot, as you and I so often do. His pursuit was self-preservation. It was more important to him to blend in with the crowd than be known as "one of those people."

Earlier I mentioned that Peter received the keys to the kingdom. I mentioned it in such a way as not to make him look foolish or to condemn him but rather to highlight the amazing grace of Jesus. Jesus knew that Peter would deny Him. Jesus is God and therefore possessed all the foreknowledge of His Father. He not only predicted Peter's denial (Mark 14:27–31); Jesus knew that one day He would honor Peter despite it (Matthew 16:19). And He does the same for us.

Tragically, you and I deny Christ every time we care more about what others think of us than of what God has already declared. Every time we seek man's approval and praise, we say to the Lord that His sacrifice was not enough. And He says to us that He became "fear of man" so that we would be counted as righteous. We are presented before the Lord as concerned only with loving and pleasing Him—and it is finished because of Christ. He is already pleased with you and with me.

There's another troubling problem with the fear of man, one that we might not give much thought to, and that is judgment. The fear of man isn't always our denial of another or our attempt to impress; we can fear man in our private thoughts about them. Our made-up scenarios and fear can lead to judging others.

Slander, Judgment, and the Fear of Man

I can remember an incident when I heard my name and personhood slammed. It was pretty terrible. It hurt. I went into the room and immediately confronted those responsible. I cried, they confessed, and that was that. They asked for forgiveness, and I forgave.

We don't typically learn what others *really* think of us. And I often wonder if we really want to know. Most of the time we're left to assume the best or nothing at all. Unfortunately, though, many of us don't assume the best or nothing at all. We're preoccupied by the opinions of others. This is the fear of man. It can show up in a variety of forms, but there's one thing we can be certain of—it's a snare (Proverbs 29:25). I've discovered that when I'm tempted to fear man, it's usually rooted in fear of what someone else thinks of me. But as I dig deeper, I realize that I'm actually judging and assuming the worst of *them*.

Fear of Man and Judgment

The fear of man so often ends with judging others, because we begin to assume we know another's motives, thoughts, character, and intentions. Someone forgets to answer an email, so you assume you're not a priority and that she is selfish. It turns out she was on vacation. You pass someone in the hall, and he doesn't wave, so you assume he doesn't like you or is rude. It turns out he didn't see you. You invite someone to do something, and she kindly declines, so you assume she's disappointed in you. It turns out she simply doesn't want to attend or is sick or tied up. It really doesn't matter what the other person thinks or does, but our preoccupation with worrying about what others think of us drives us to sinfully judge.

Fear of Man and Self-Forgetfulness

The false thoughts leading us to judge others are a form of pride that can only be remedied by what Tim Keller calls "gospel humility." As he explains in his helpful book *The Freedom of Self-Forgetfulness*:

> Gospel humility is not needing to think about myself. Not needing to connect things with myself. It is an end to thoughts such as, "I'm in this room with these people, does that make me look good? Do I want to be here?" True gospel humility means I stop connecting every experience, every conversation, with myself. In fact, I stop thinking about myself. The freedom of self-forgetfulness. The blessed rest that only self-forgetfulness brings.[2]

Preoccupation with what others think is pride. Perhaps you long to be highly regarded. Maybe you hate the idea of being misunderstood (oh, how I relate). Whatever else it is, it's pride, and we know God opposes the proud (James 4:6).

Every true believer longs for gospel humility. None of us wishes to stay as we are—we want to be transformed into Christlikeness. Christians don't desire to disobey God and grieve the Spirit. Besides, it's no fun being consumed by what you think someone else thinks. Keller shares the secret to the sweet forgetfulness that we find in the gospel:

> Do you realize that it is only in the gospel of Jesus Christ that you get the verdict before the performance? . . . In Christianity, the verdict leads to performance. It is not the performance that leads to the verdict. In Christianity, the moment we believe, God says, "This is my beloved son in whom I am well pleased." Or take Romans 8:1, which says, "Therefore, there is now no condemnation for those who are in Christ Jesus." In Christianity, the moment we believe, God imputes Christ's perfect performance to us as if it were our own, and adopts us into his family. In other words, God can say to us just as he once said to Christ, "You are my Son, whom I love; with you I am well pleased."[3]

The verdict of "well done" is in, and as a result you and I run the race of faith, putting off judgment and the fear of man. Even though we will fail miserably, we make the effort nonetheless. After all, God's "well done" motivates and inspires a life consecrated to His glory.

I wish I could say that the fight against fear of man and the temptation to judge others is easy. But it isn't. We can be assured, though, that God will indeed finish the good work

He began in us (Philippians 1:6). This is a walk of faith, a race to the finish line that will lead us out of our struggle with sin and temptation and into glory. One day we will be with our Savior, worshiping Him forever. We'll never again worship the idol of man.

A Crossroads

When I first heard the good news of the gospel, it was so marvelous and freeing that I couldn't help but rejoice and share it with others. (Have you noticed that about new Christians?) But in what seemed like a moment's time, my joy and carefree spirit became gripped by the fear of man. I was so afraid I was doing something wrong all the time. I had feared man before, but at this time it wasn't hidden from me. It was staring me in the face. There was a short season when I thought I had mastered the beast. I read books (similar to this chapter) entirely dedicated to the topic. I prayed. I did all these things, and it seemed to be working. But then I got married. I remember situation after situation when I feared what my husband thought of me. Did he think my figure was shapely enough? Was I too shapely? What did he think of my cooking? Was my food up to his mother's standards? (She's a gourmet chef without the title or the accolades.) It was a never-ending battle. He would thank me for making a meal but not in the way I hoped, so I just assumed he hated it. I'd feel deflated. Me, me, me. It was all about me.

Unfortunately, it didn't end there. My fear of what others thought of me began to affect my marriage. My husband would reassure me and encourage me about various pursuits, and yet I feared what other women thought. Women would share their opinions, and instead of weighing their words against God's Word and trusting the Lord (and my husband), I would become paralyzed by fear. I'd second-guess his decisions, thinking about what others would or wouldn't do. I hated the thought of not being accepted because I was "different."

As I already noted, the fear of man is described in God's Word as a snare (Proverbs 29:25). A snare is a trap. It traps you in your mind and keeps you from obeying, trusting, and fearing the Lord. It is a trap that kept me from trusting my husband with decisions or his word. It is a snare because it traps you into elevating people above God—people become your object of worship.

I found myself at a crossroads. Either I could believe that what God said in His Word about His children is true, or I could continue to trust my own feelings, fears, and thoughts. It was a matter of faith. God says He is for us (Romans 8:31); He views those in Christ as covered in Christ's righteousness (Romans 5:17); and He is working in our life (Philippians 1:6). God was humbling me so that He might lift me up.

The remedy for the fear of man isn't a greater view or love of self. As I said in *United*,

> The world's prescription for the cure of the fear of man is to find ways to be proud of oneself and find security in and through the self. Quotes like "Love yourself" or "Believe in yourself" or even the sweet but theologically lame quote widely attributed to Walt Disney, "If you can dream it, you can do it," are all focused on self. But God says that the opposite of

the fear of man isn't finding security and pride in one-self. No, it's placing one's trust and security in Him.[4]

Killing the fear of man is rooted in, as Tim Keller says (borrowing from C. S. Lewis), thinking of yourself less.[5]

For you and me to stop worrying about others, we have to start thinking about Him. As we meditate on the character of God and remember His holiness (Psalm 77:13), omniscience (Psalm 147:5), sovereignty (Deuteronomy 4:39), and love (John 3:16), we begin to experience the beginning of wisdom and understanding (Psalm 111:10). When I began to intentionally think about God's character, I started to experience true freedom in Christ and joy in the Lord. My life was no longer partly dependent on others; it was more fully submitted to God.

Again, it isn't that I think less of myself. I don't fight the fear of man and my concern about what others think by assuming the worst about everything I do and beating myself up while elevating others. I don't deny God's gifts in my life, which would be false humility. I don't walk around with my head down in fear of praise or encouragement either, which would only draw more attention to myself. What I am learning to do is forget about myself so that I can enjoy others and enjoy what the Lord is doing and, most importantly, enjoy and worship my Father.

You may not struggle to the severity that I have, but I don't doubt you've found yourself in situations where you were concerned about what others think of you. It is so easy to do. I believe one reason we care so much about what others think is a desire to preserve an image. We want others to think we are carefree or "cool," so we disobey the Lord in a certain area; we want others to think we are righteous, so we play the good-girl role even when we are miserable; we want others to think we don't associate with that person or that organization, so we ignore friends (like Peter ignored Jesus). Our actions keep us from loving and serving others, often because we just care so much about what others think. We do this because of pride. Our pride and desire to be seen a certain way prevent us from living the life God desires for us.

So the real question is, do you struggle with finding your full and complete acceptance and satisfaction in God alone? I do, and I'm sure you do too. Everyone does to varying degrees. But if you relate to what I've written and sense a deep longing to be accepted by others, you may find yourself experiencing despair. You simply won't be able to please people. It can't be done. We can please others but only to a certain degree, and it won't satisfy. Their praise will only leave us hungry for more. Their affection will leave us wanting. Their acceptance will run out when they sin against us, and we discover they are sinful too. The only thing that will ever satisfy us without disappointment is the Lord.

We can't find true, lasting pleasure and satisfaction except through and by Him. David understood this, and he wrote, "You make known to me the path of life; in your presence there is fullness of joy; at your right hand are pleasures forevermore" (Psalm 16:11). We trade these pleasures, which are forevermore, for the hope of acceptance or praise that lasts a minute and is from mere mortals. When you think about it that way, it's clear that it's a worthless pursuit.

The problem with dwelling too long here is that we can

be in danger of becoming too introspective. The point isn't to make you feel sorry for yourself. That's not the goal, and it's not the spirit of self-forgetfulness. What you and I need to do is remember God. We don't have to run after pleasing people, because there is one who is already pleased with us. The blood of Jesus covers the fear of man. God looks on you as righteous, as if you fear Him perfectly. You and I can't preach this to ourselves enough, because we so easily forget. God has the power to change you and me—He will complete His good work.

A Safe Place

Proverbs 29:25 says that those who fear man are ensnared but that those who do not fear man trust the Lord and are safe. In other words, the fear of man reflects a heart that does not trust the Lord. Peter didn't trust that the Lord would protect him, and when I fear what others think, I don't trust that the Lord is pleased with me. But God is after our heart and mind. He wants us to love Him with all our heart and with all our mind (Matthew 23:37). He wants us to trust Him. In Him alone there is peace, rest, and safety.

It's so familiar to hear about how much the Lord forgives sin, and perhaps that's the ultimate expression of His safety (safety from His wrath), but rarely do we talk about this aspect of His character. There is safety in God. You and I think we have to be in control of how we are viewed or of what others think, but God says no, we are safe. We think we need to worry about the harm others could inflict, physical or otherwise, so we withhold speaking about Jesus; but God says no, we are safe. The fear of man leads us into a trap, like a caged animal, but the fear of the Lord leads us into the arms of a safe Father. How amazing is that? In chapter 9 we will dive deep into what it means to fear the Lord, but right now just be in awe that you are safe in the Lord.

Perhaps this is your first time facing the fear of man for what it is. As I mentioned before, the Lord desires that we not remain as we are. You and I don't want to be like the man who looks in the mirror and forgets what he looks like (James 1:23–24). If God is bringing the sweet grace of conviction, He will provide the sweet grace of escape, forgiveness, and repentance. Ask God to give you a vision for who He is, and then trust that He is who He says He is. You are safe in Him.

———— ◆ ————

My father passed away my freshman year of college. He battled juvenile diabetes most of his life, and, in the end, cancer and congestive heart failure took him to his final resting place. He was my hero and best friend. The Lord used his life to protect me from much, and He used his death as a means to reveal Himself to me. I no longer had my dad to live for. Upon becoming a Christian, it became so clear to me that God wanted me to understand that He is my Father. And though I sin against the Lord, I don't disappoint Him, because He isn't looking at my performance—He is looking at Jesus. This is remarkable. As His daughter I do want to please Him and give Him the honor due His name, but I do not have to fear His rejection or anger (wrath). This is our Father, ladies. Let this motivate you not to fear another.

Chapter 2

FEAR OF
THE FUTURE

My husband's job takes him away on trips that last a few days or even a week at a time. Each time he leaves, I battle the fear that he will never return. He boards a flight, and I imagine the plane bursting into flames. He rents a car, and I pray he doesn't get into a car accident. The truth is, these things *could* happen (okay, the plane isn't likely to burst into flames, but go with me). I know women who have lost husbands in car accidents; I know there are times when people walk out the door for something routine and never return; but I can't live constantly worrying about a future that hasn't happened.

I'm not sure if there is a greater fear for women than the fear of what's to come (or what won't come). You and I rightly pray for our husband, children, schools, and whether to pursue a career, but we don't often come to God in peace. Instead we come anxiously awaiting our fate. Goodness will follow all the days of *her* life, or *her* life, or maybe *her* life, we might think, but surely not *my* life. It's hard not to have control, and one thing that we can't ever determine is what lies ahead. Thankfully, God's Word is packed with sweet promises that smash all our fearful thinking.

Imagine, if you will, that you are ninety years old. You are most likely frail with gray hair, potentially walking with a cane, though perhaps, these days, spending much of your time in a wheelchair because your once able and strong legs have ceased to perform. Now imagine someone comes to you and says, "Hey, Sarah, you know that child you've always wanted? Well, it's time. You are finally going to bear a child." You would look at that person in absolute disbelief. You might even laugh. All these years of waiting and longing and then, when every shred of hope is gone, a son is promised.

I am referring to the story of God's promise of Isaac to Abraham and Sarah. In the pages of Genesis we read of how God promised Abraham a legacy of nations through the birth of one son (Genesis 17:16). Abraham and Sarah laughed in doubt as they heard God's declaration (Genesis 17:17; 18:12). Sarah, I imagine, must have desired children prior to God's promise. There's a host of fears associated with the chance that you might not become pregnant, and, I would guess by her doubtful laugh, she had given up at the age of ninety on the prospect of ever conceiving. Could you imagine actually becoming pregnant at ninety?

With a rhetorical question God challenged Sarah to trust Him, after she had defiantly laughed in doubt that she would become pregnant: "Is anything too hard for the LORD?" (Genesis 18:14). God fulfilled His promise, and Sarah miraculously became pregnant. But once she did become pregnant, she had nine months of waiting to see how her frail, weak body would respond. Would she be able to carry the baby to term? By means of a miscarriage would God teach her a lesson about trusting Him? I don't know about you, but those are some of the thoughts I might battle after becoming pregnant at ninety. I would struggle with fear of the unknown. I would want to be in complete control of the situation. Perhaps I would struggle because I've had some of these fears come to fruition. I have experienced four miscarriages and have had to fight the fear of losing a child through each pregnancy. Later, in chapter 4, I'll share more about this experience.

You might be thinking, *Yes, but everything turned out exactly the way these biblical characters hoped.* Yes and no. Sarah would have loved to have had a child at a younger age (I assume). She died at 127 years old, leaving Abraham a mourning widower, never getting to see her son Isaac marry (Genesis 23:1; 24). And as we know, life continued to be difficult for her descendants. Did it turn out the way the Lord planned? Absolutely! And does God redeem it in the end? Yes. But you can't see the future in your own life like you get to in God's Word. We don't get the whole picture, do we? So we have to trust the Lord because only He knows. But there is one thing guaranteed, which is awaiting you all the days of your life: God's faithfulness.

Those words—God has been faithful and will be again—appear in the lyrics of "He's Always Been Faithful" by Sara Groves. In the song she recounts God's faithfulness through each morning and each season. She recounts, "Season by season, I watch Him amazed; in awe of the mysteries of His perfect ways."[1] Every page in God's Word shouts of the faithfulness of God. Each story leads to Jesus and to the redemption of the world. And if we look, we can see God's faithfulness to us now.

In Deuteronomy 32:4, Moses speaks of God as the "Rock" whose works are "perfect" and ways are "justice." He is "a God of faithfulness and without iniquity, just and upright is he." And we read in 1 Thessalonians 5:24 of Paul's confidence in the faithfulness of God: "He who calls you is faithful; he will surely do it." And elsewhere Paul writes that God will finish the good work He began in us (Philippians 1:6). Psalm 89, though a lament, still sings of God's faithfulness: "I will sing of the steadfast love of the LORD, forever; with my mouth I will make known your faithfulness to all generations. . . . O LORD God of hosts, who is mighty as you are, O LORD, with your faithfulness all around you?" (vv. 1, 8).

You and I have to fight to remember the faithfulness of our Father when we are faced with great fears of the future. Ask yourself, how has God been faithful? This year you can count on the Lord to be faithful again. This doesn't mean that everything will turn out exactly as you desire. This doesn't mean each prayer will be answered as you wish. But it does mean that in God's goodness and sovereignty, He will work all things together as He sees them to be good for you (Romans 8:28). We may not see the evidence of God's faithful hand until the end of our days, but we know it will be there.

Until that day when our faith becomes sight, we will continue to struggle. I think there are two reasons I tend to fear the future. The first is that I believe I know what is best for my family and me. I am convinced that I would do what is best, and therefore I want to take control. During these times, I do not trust that the Lord knows best, and I do not trust that He is operating as my Father. What we all need, I think to myself, is peace, perfect health, wealth, and comfort. We need a life of ease and not sorrow. These are not bad things to desire in and of themselves. As a matter of fact, much of this dream life I hope for is what I will one day receive in heaven. Life is hard and difficult because we live in a fallen world. Once sin entered, there was a noticeable toil to life and work.

But what happens when I fear for the worst about our future? What happens when I see that I might be in danger of receiving these hard things? My temptation is to get anxious and filled with worry. Anxiety can lead to irrational behavior. I remember one particular day when I was worried about my husband. I sat on my couch waiting for him to call. He was out of town on business, and I wanted to make sure he had arrived safely. I called his cellphone, and there was no answer. After thirty minutes of silence, I imagined he must be busy and continued on with my day. A few hours passed, and I began to worry. Did he get robbed? Did the plane go down in a ball of flames? (Me and planes? So, my fear of flying isn't obvious or anything!) My mind began to wander, and assumptions and fears poured in. Then the phone rang. "Hi, Babe," he said in his usual calm and collected voice. "I'm so sorry I didn't call you. My phone died, and I've just now settled into the hotel."

Did all my worrying do anyone any good? Nope. And, thankfully, God has something to say about this. In Matthew 6:27, Jesus asks, "Which of you by being anxious can add a single hour to his span of life?" The answer is simple—no one adds anything to his or her life by worrying about the future. Jesus is addressing our not being anxious about our lives, and much of what He addresses has to do with the future: "Do not be anxious about your life, what you *will* eat or what you *will* drink, nor about your body, what you *will* put on" (Matthew 6:25).

The second reason I fear the future is, I think, unbelief. All fear has an element of unbelief, but the fear of what will happen in one's future seems especially derived from a lack of faith. Since God is real and powerful and good, why wouldn't I rest in the unknown? It's because, during those moments when I feel that everything is out of control, I believe God isn't who He says He is and that I must take matters into my own hands. Essentially I'm saying that God can't handle this mess. He can't handle this concern. He can't handle this potential disaster, so I need to try to fix it through worrying or actions that may not be necessary.

My concern with the future typically involves health and the safety of my family, but yours may be something else. Perhaps your fear of the future involves losing your home, finances, or job, so, because of your fear, you lack faith in God's provision, so you store up treasures on earth (Matthew 6:19–21) and do not give financially. Maybe your fear is divorce, so you are tempted to mistrust your husband. There is an endless list of ways we can be tempted to doubt that God can really handle the future.

I imagine that the father of the boy with an unclean spirit didn't have a glowing view of the future for his son. Mark records that the young boy had a spirit in him that made him mute, threw him down, and caused his mouth to foam (Mark

9:17–18). The father brought the boy to Jesus' disciples, who were unable to heal the kid, so he turned to Jesus, who immediately rebuked everyone, saying, "O faithless generation, how long am I to be with you?" (Mark 9:19). The people had the same problem we do—unbelief. But even with doubt, the father continued to plead with Jesus to heal his son. The father said, "I believe; help my unbelief!" (Mark 9:24). He didn't know what the future would hold for his son, but he knew enough to know that Jesus had the power to save him. He didn't come to Jesus with a mountain of faith—he had little faith. This should encourage us as we struggle with our own doubts and fears of the future. Even a little faith can protect us from the unnecessary worry and anxiety produced by fear. Though we doubt God can handle it all, He can, and we will see why and how in chapter 8.

For now, know that God wants to remind us that He will take care of all our needs. We don't have to fear the future. "Are not two sparrows sold for a penny? And not one of them will fall to the ground apart from your Father" (Matthew 10:29). The only thing that will remedy our fearful, controlling, hungry, anxious hearts is understanding, knowing, and finding more of Him. We need to know that He is good, in control, and mindful of man. All the while, we cry out to the Lord, "I believe; help my unbelief!"

Chapter 3

FEAR OF OTHER WOMEN

One hindrance to the sweet ministry of Titus 2 and the community in which God intended for the church is sinful comparison. Blame it on social media. Blame it on magazines. Whatever you want to blame it on, it's real and it's ugly. *What she has is better. Why can't I have that? I only wish . . .* You know what I'm talking about. It's that nagging desire for something that someone else has, which is rooted in covetousness. This transforms into a fear of women who seem better, greater, or more put together. Or, worse, this fear can lead us to slander, gossip, or speak disparagingly about them under our breath. We need to put off covetousness and put on rejoicing, love, and contentment.

One of my favorite writers, Elyse Fitzpatrick, wrote a book called *Women Helping Women*.[1] Let me say right off that I've never read it (I've read plenty of her other books), although I have met Elyse. She is probably one of the most honest women I've ever known. She is raw and real and funny. And, honestly, this chapter has nothing to do with her at all. But the title of her book simply made me think of the problem I see often in our churches and sisterhood. Women, we don't seem to be helping each other. And, actually, it would appear we are getting really good at hating one another. I know that sounds strong, but when I look on the Internet, that's what I read.

I find that we're tough on each other. There's a phenomenon that we've actually named the "Mommy Wars." We debate about how to feed and train our children. Is it organic, whole foods, or canned? We give birth at the hospital, or we do it at home—and further, you aren't even a real woman if you haven't experienced natural birth! And don't get me started on homeschooling versus public school. We could lose friendships by making that decision the "wrong" way.

It's popular to speak about the ways men have oppressed us as women, and yet I'm left wondering: are men really the problem? I just don't think so. Men aren't leading this war. And even if you've never fully engaged in it, you probably know what I'm talking about. Here's a few more: women who work are accused of being independent feminists, women who stay home are wasting their gifts, women who do both are ignoring their children, women should breastfeed, babies should sleep with their parents, young girls should go to college, young girls should think solely about marriage, and on and on. Women who are excited about the Lord—criticized by their sisters? It's exhausting.

Surely we know that we are the ones doing the hurting, don't we? We know this, right?

———— ◆ ————

I was chatting with some of my girlfriends recently about blog ideas. One of them said, "I want to start a blog called 'I'm a Loser Mom.'" We all laughed and then started talking about how different our actual lives look compared to our Facebook lives. We joked about getting up later than we wished, posting Instagram pictures of our messy rooms, feeding our kids sugary cereals for breakfast, and popping in a movie one too many times.

Do you ever feel like a loser mom? If so, you're in good company. We all feel like losers at times. Knowing this will allow us not to grovel in self-pity but instead relate to one another. We can love one another rather than compete or envy when we realize that we are all in this together. Really. Not one of us has it together. This is good news, friends.

Now, there are definitely days when I wake up at 5 a.m. and get a lot done, the kids are obedient, I'm able to read my Bible, and I work out. But because life is hectic, kids are unpredictable, sickness comes, cars break down, hormones rage, and schedules collide, sometimes my life looks like a tornado blew through—and my home reflects it. I'm not saying there isn't peace and grace in the chaos; I'm simply saying life doesn't always look as perfect as we depict (or desire).

We don't need to succumb to the pressures to be magazine perfect—you know, like the *Southern Living* style homes, Martha Stewart table settings, and Food Network meals. Magazine perfection is an illusion. Every publication employs talented artists whose sole duty is to manipulate the images to present something that isn't quite real. I've been in commercials, and it's not real. (I was once in a commercial for the Knoxville area bus line—yes, the bus company—and I was the ticket agent. Giggle.) As just one example, the food (though it looks great) is fake. And if it is real, there have been a few "takes" to get it just right. Photoshop can make anything look fabulous.

There is nothing wrong with the pursuit of all things diligent, organized, and hardworking. The Lord commends the hard worker. Proverbs 18:9 warns that "whoever is slack in his work is a brother to him who destroys." When I wake up in the morning I'm not thinking, *I want today to be chaotic.* Life just works out that way sometimes. We must aim to glorify the Lord in all we do and rest in the Savior, who doesn't place on us pressures for perfection.

Ladies, here's the good news: you aren't a loser. You are made in the image of God (Genesis 1:26), you are fearfully and wonderfully made (Psalm 139:14), and the Lord rejoices over you with gladness (Zephaniah 3:17). He doesn't look at you and determine whether He will accept you based on your practices. He looks at His Son. How freeing is that?

Aren't these truths about the Lord's delight much better to meditate on than *Southern Living* ads or the latest recipe or design project on Pinterest, or what you see your sister doing or not doing on social media? Next time I look at my messy living room, which I did intend to clean but instead tended to the immediate needs of my children, I'll think of God's delight over me. And as I seek after Him and His kingdom, He will give me all I need (Matthew 6:33; 13:44).

Begrudging Your Sister

Now, it would behoove me to say that some women really do seem to be able to juggle much and still live with joy. Unfortunately I have seen these women labeled as "Stepford wives." The term *Stepford wife* refers to a docile woman who cooks, cleans, organizes her home, obeys her husband, and dresses nicely. She has it all together. But she doesn't have personality.

Unfortunately this caricature can be attributed to any woman who appears to have it all together. We cry out against the woman who cooks a nice meal or talks kindly about her kids. Surely she is putting on a mask, we assume. In our fear of being judged as lazy or of incurring the Lord's disapproval, one way we might seek to feel better about ourselves is to mock other women. Yet have we ever stepped back to consider that some woman have been especially gifted by God as cheerful, thankful homemakers?

We are all given the same Spirit but different gifts. Paul teaches us about this variety of gifts in 1 Corinthians 12. This is important for you and me to remember when we walk into a friend's clean and organized home or enjoy her tasty cooking and cheerful spirit, or when we view a friend's social media post with her perfectly coiffed hair and smiling children in matching outfits. God made us all in His image, but we are unique. He variously gifts us to serve for the benefit of others.

Yet we're tempted to judge (Matthew 7:1–5), so we assume these women must be hypocrites; or we become jealous and compare (we do not have, so we covet; Exodus 20:17). If that is your temptation, know that you are not alone. In fact, God's Word says temptation is common to man (1 Corinthians 10:13). But you don't have to give in to this temptation. What if you rejoiced instead? Perhaps if you see women who excel in areas you do not, it can be used as an opportunity to thank God for His creative design.

All Good Gifts

It's difficult to rejoice when you are struggling. I know. But if God calls us to "rejoice with those who rejoice" (Romans 12:15), He will give us the grace to do it. During those tough times of comparing and judging, which are potentially rooted in fear, we must run fast to the throne of grace to receive help in our time of need (Hebrews 4:16). We can also run far away from temptation. We can avoid Instagram and Facebook (you can do it!), but we can't always flee our cheerful friends. In other words, we need to ask God for help to change our hearts. We want to look at the log in our own eye rather than focus on the speck in our sisters'. I believe we can, by the power of the Spirit, rejoice with those who rejoice. We can be excited for others and see God's good work.

Ultimately, you and I must fix our eyes on Jesus. He is the *only* cure for our temptations. When you are looking at your friend thinking, Why can't I do what she's doing? Why don't I have her capacity? you can thank God that He never required you to have her capacity. You need only to work in the strength God has supplied you. He is the source. He is the giver of all good things.

God may not have gifted you the same way as your neighbor or the woman online who decorates elaborate cakes every night or the mom who has young kids and a clean home (seems like an oxymoron, I know!). Remember the source of her gifts and yours. This will cause you to rejoice—not in the gift but in the Giver. God has truly made us all equal in value and worth, but with varying gifts. And, as with salvation, none may boast (1 Corinthians 1:26–31), because all good gifts come from God.

Fight Fear through Encouragement

I prefer not to bring up what I see as a glaring problem without thinking of a few solutions. I thank God that He encourages us to put off sin and guard against temptation but doesn't leave us to figure out what to put on (Colossians 3:1–17), and that, to me, is encouragement.

Without the kind encouragement of my friends, my church, my pastors, my husband, and my co-laborers, I think I'd have given up on much of what I do. There is a reenergizing and faith-building effect of encouragement. And I'm not talking about a passing word from a friend ("You look nice today"). I'm thinking of specific, direct, detailed encouragement, encouragement that is pointed and gracious. Encouragement points out the ways God is moving in the lives of others. Thus encouragement points others toward God.

We looked at the fear of man in chapter 1. One symptom of the fear of man is flattery. We can tell people what we think they want to hear in hopes of getting something from them. That is not encouragement. Encouragement isn't about us, and it really isn't about the person receiving it either. Rather, it's about the Lord and the grace of God that you see in her life.

And as with all things, Christ is our supreme example of encouragement. He is our example for loving those who walk differently. He is our example for bearing with one another. Paul writes:

> We who are strong have an obligation to bear with the failings of the weak, and not to please ourselves. Let each of us please his neighbor for his good, to build him up. For Christ did not please himself, but as it is written, "The reproaches of those who reproached you fell on me." For whatever was written in former days was written for our instruction, that through endurance and through the encouragement of the Scriptures we might have hope. May the God of endurance and encouragement grant you to live in such harmony with one another, in accord with Christ Jesus, that together you may with one voice glorify the God and Father of our Lord Jesus Christ. Therefore welcome one another as Christ has welcomed you, for the glory of God. (Romans 15:1–7)

I love how the *ESV Study Bible* expounds on verse 7: "Therefore, in conclusion, both the strong and the weak are exhorted to accept one another, for they have been accepted by Christ even though they are sinners. Such mutual acceptance will bring great glory to God."[2] The "weak" Paul is referring to there are those who felt the need to "keep the law" (see Romans 14). But for us modern-day women, I think we can include anyone who thinks differently than we do. There is much more that can and should be said regarding these verses; I'm seriously skimming over the surface. I don't want to detract from the main point—fearing other women can lead to begrudging, comparing, and failing to encourage.

Band of Sisters

I've never seen the HBO miniseries *Band of Brothers*. I do know that it is a depiction of men fighting during World War II. The title brings to mind a squadron of men with the same frame of mind—to win the war—coming together as a unified front. They aren't just men at war; they are brothers on a quest together, bound by their mission.

Now imagine if we had this mentality in us as we relate to our sisters in Christ. Imagine if we banded together with one voice proclaiming that Christ is enough and then proclaiming to our sisters the same—"Christ is enough!" Wow! How powerful that would be. I want you to know that Christ is enough. Those familiar verses and words about the Lord's rejoicing over you aren't to make you feel better. They are the truth.

So let's look for ways to build each other up and to spur each other on in love. For we know that our flesh and heart may fail us, but we also know that God is our strength and portion forevermore (Psalm 73:26). Let's draw upon that strength to point others to Him, the one who is able to make our sister stand firm (Romans 14:4).

We can put on encouragement because of what is written in Titus 3:3–7:

> For we ourselves were once foolish, disobedient, led astray, slaves to various passions and pleasures, passing our days in malice and envy, hated by others and hating one another. But when the goodness

and loving kindness of God our Savior appeared, he saved us, not because of works done by us in righteousness, but according to his own mercy, by the washing of regeneration and renewal of the Holy Spirit, whom he poured out on us richly through Jesus Christ our Savior, so that being justified by his grace we might become heirs according to the hope of eternal life.

We were once filled with malice, envy, and hate, but now, because of Jesus, we can resist falling into those sins. The temptation will remain, but because of His goodness and lovingkindness Jesus appeared and saved us—He made us new. Because we are new, we can fight sin. Because we are His, we desire to fight it (otherwise we would find a way to justify our thoughts and behavior). God does the work of making us new, which includes creating in us a new heart that desires to love and do good to our neighbor. We can rest in knowing that He provides the means to fight and the grace to love. He will help us rejoice with and encourage our sisters.

Chapter 4

FEAR OF TRAGEDY

The fear of tragedy is my greatest fear, so this chapter will be deeply personal. It's my greatest fear because it's something I know and understand. I've experienced tragedy, and even as the Lord continues to teach me, I still battle with this temptation to fear. I experienced four miscarriages, and with each pregnancy I faced new and surprising fears. My father passed away at the young age of fifty-two, leaving four daughters and a brokenhearted wife. My oldest sister died suddenly of congestive heart failure at the age of forty. All devastating tragedies. Our personal history powerfully impacts what and how we fear. But even if we've never had anything tragic happen, everyone to one degree or another can struggle with the fear of tragedy, whether it involves loss (death, possessions, money) or otherwise.

Much of my fear of the future is really a fear of *potential* tragedy. It becomes clockwork for me. My husband doesn't pick up my call on the way home from work, and by the time he arrives home, I have planned his funeral and all but thought through how I will care for two small children by myself. The thought of getting pregnant again, though welcome, always leaves me wondering in the back of my head: *Will this young baby survive in my womb?* And if I have a sickness for any prolonged period, I can fight thoughts of my children being without a mother. This is fear. Sinful fear. It is sinful because it is a lack of faith and trust in God. Essentially, as I've mentioned, it is a form of unbelief. My heart wants control because, if I'm honest, I'd like to never experience pain again. I want to be like the Christians who ask God for trials in order to strengthen their faith, but my faith wanes in this area of asking. This sort of unbelief, not believing that God is good in all He does, blinds me when I'm tempted to fear tragedy.

Do you ever experience this gripping fear—a fear that is almost paralyzing? I don't know of anyone who wasn't frightened when the Twin Towers came crashing down into a pile of rubble and ashes on that fateful day we now call 9/11. The aftermath of that day led many to become fearful of flying. Some abandoned flying altogether and took to the road, which unfortunately didn't help their statistical chances of survival.[1] It is statistically proven that driving is far more dangerous than flying. Even still, we fear flying, and tragedies such as 9/11 don't help ease that fear. Thankfully we have God's Word to help us when we are confused and made afraid by the world.

Ruth's Story

When we are in the middle of a trial, it's easy to be nearsighted. We focus on solving the problem or dealing with the trauma rather than on the future good that could come from the trial, like, for example, when we are admitted into a hospital. At such times we understandably focus on the when/where/how of that particular time. The future, which we can't see, involves the nurse with whom we were able to share the gospel while we waited and recovered. Our near-sightedness won't allow us to see the future grace, and we can never really know what to expect—except that God is good. This is just one example of what can happen.

When we fear tragedy that hasn't even happened, unlike the miscarriages I endured, we put ourselves through unnecessary stress. That's why our Lord tells us not to worry about tomorrow, because today has enough trouble of its own (Matthew 6:34). And it's so true. Each day often does come with its variety of trials, but when we worry about things that aren't there, we are creating more trouble for ourselves. That's why there's something comforting about hearing other people's stories. Their stories can help provide comfort. And at times it is good to be reminded that we are not alone. We are not alone in our struggle with sin and temptation. Perhaps that's why God's Word includes so many verses addressing how we should relate to one another. We need each other, especially in times of trials, if only to hear about the faithfulness of God. We don't get to see the end of our own trial at the beginning of it—the future grace that will inevitably come from a trial. But when we get the chance to sit down with a friend and hear how the Lord was faithful in her trial, our faith is built.

This is how I feel when I read through the book of Ruth. At the beginning, everything looks bleak and hopeless for Ruth and her family. There is a famine in their hometown of

Bethlehem, so they leave and travel to Moab. While there, the husband of Ruth's mother-in-law, Naomi, dies, leaving Naomi a widow with her two sons, who die ten years after the death of their father. Naomi is now left without her husband and her two sons. Perhaps this specific scenario is one that you can't seem to relate to. Not too many people experience such a trial, but my grandmother did. Her husband passed away, and both her sons, who were in their fifties, died within a few years. My grandmother, now in her eighties, had a trial almost identical to Naomi's: widowed and left with two daughters-in-law.

We can at times distance ourselves from these biblical stories. They seem extreme—an elderly woman like Sarah having a baby, a man like Job losing everything he owns and his entire family, generations being wiped out, etc. These things do indeed also happen now, as in my grandmother's life. There really isn't anything new under the sun. How do we benefit from knowing this when we are faced with fear?

Naomi assumed she would be alone. I imagine that she wrestled with fear, like many women would. What would she do on her own? Where would she go? She urged her daughters to leave her and return to their mothers' homes (Ruth 1:8). One did obey Naomi's pleas to leave her, but Ruth clung to her and refused to leave her side (Ruth 1:14). We know that the end of what seemed to be a hopeless, tragic series of events had a great purpose. The Lord had a plan to redeem the situation and ultimately the whole world. Ruth met and married Boaz and had a child named Obed. Obed is the grandfather of King David, and we begin to see the lineage of our Savior Jesus (Ruth 4:13–22).

Naomi and Ruth didn't see the end before the beginning. God was faithful and kind to the women. He fulfilled His great purposes for their lives. There is no guarantee that we will not experience a similar trial (remember my grandmother), but we can rest in knowing that if and when tragedy strikes, we don't need to fear. We are in the hands of a mighty God who is able to do more than we could ever imagine or dream. God is for us and not against us (Romans 8:31), and we will get to the goodness of God in His sovereignty in the chapters ahead. The point is that our fear of tragedy can be rooted in a fear of suffering and not having control. The good news is that we have a God who is in control and knows what is best for us. He promises good—not a lack of trial but ultimate good. We neither need to, nor should we, worry in fear about future tragic events. What the story of Ruth helps remind us is, if we do fall into the temptation to fear, that God is good.

Later we will explore how to respond when bad things do happen, because they do. We can guarantee that we will lose someone we love dearly—perhaps that is your fear. But we don't have to walk with one eye looking over our shoulder waiting for the Lord to rain down terror. That isn't the character of our God, and He doesn't want us to live in such a way. We can instead join David and proclaim, "My eyes are ever toward the Lord, for he will pluck my feet out of the net" (Psalm 25:15). We can have confidence that God is for us and with us. This is the lesson I am learning.

I realize that my temptation, as many of yours may be, is to try to hold on to what is most precious. My husband and kids are most precious to me, and therefore I fear losing them. Makes sense. What I need to be aware of, though, is that this could be a sign of an idol in my life. Perhaps my fear of losing them, which leads to sinful and unnecessary anxiety, is because I want them too much. They are mini gods. Idolatry is something to consider as you and I fight fear.

Trusting the Lord with my future and the future of my husband and children is one of the most difficult exercises of my faith. No one desires that their family experience harm. The Lord is teaching me to remember the stories of His faithfulness in the life of others, like Ruth, and in my own life. And as we will see in the final chapters, I fight fear by remembering the wisdom and character of God. God is good, gracious, and loving as well as sovereign. I *can* trust Him. My fears subside as I remember and throw myself into His capable arms.

My husband's work trips have become easier (not easy). The most noticeable change has been a sense of peace rather than anxiety when he leaves. When he walks out the door, my face no longer looks slightly terrified. I can send him off in faith, kiss his sweet lips, and wear a genuine smile. It is the same with my children. My kids' futures are seen as they should be—completely unknown but in the hands of my Father.

Legitimate Fear

Up to this point, we've been considering our sinful tendencies to fear tragedy. We want to guard against these fears whenever and however possible. They simply do us no good. Living without being gripped and ruled by fear is the ideal; however, we live in an evil and fallen world. We don't want to walk around suspicious and fearful of everyone around us. But there are times when fear is warranted and may even be a means of protection. Not all fear is rooted in sin. There are times when we should take great caution and be aware of our surroundings. But there are also those times when innocence and unwavering trust get in the way of better judgment. I had the unfortunate experience of learning the hard way of when to be more aware of my surroundings, even when it has seemed that there is no danger around.

I was sexually assaulted in college. I was not raped, but I was assaulted by a stranger. I was with a group of friends on a trip. We were straitlaced, and many were Christians. We all slept in a hotel room together (male and female), but the ladies had the bed, and the guys had the floor. An older man who was on the trip, but staying in another room, came in to visit. We thought it would be fine (we were naïve and young). To say the least, it wasn't okay. During the night he did something inappropriate to me that startled and woke me. Thankfully, I was in a room with many people. Others woke up and confronted him immediately. He was kicked out of school and went to jail. During the court hearing I learned that he had a wife and had molested his kids. Just awful.

Before that incident I never thought about the need to be cautious. I didn't think I needed to have a healthy fear. Caution in certain situations is wise and good, but I didn't think it was needed in this case. And let me be clear—this was not *my* fault. I feel absolutely no guilt over the situation. No one who is ever victimized in such a circumstance should feel at fault. I do, however, wish I'd had a healthy fear at the time—a healthy caution. Perhaps if I'd had greater discernment I would have returned to my room rather than spend the night in a room full of "good" boys. Temptation could have been flying all through those four walls. Although I was not at fault, I was naïve, and there's a difference. The truth is, it's difficult to write about sexual assault. First, there's the potential for becoming the perpetual victim. Then there's the real shame of being violated by another human being. But it is rampant and important to address. My seemingly innocent situation quickly turned criminal and painful.

I was young (eighteen) and immature and found myself in court helping to convict a sex offender. The aftermath for me was nothing compared to what I imagined was the aftermath for his family. I struggled with fear at night and didn't trust men for possibly one full year. God did a work of grace in my heart to forgive the perpetrator, pray for his family, and begin to trust God for my safety and security.

So if God had to help me learn to trust Him again, why does this story fall under the subhead of "Legitimate Fear"? It is not legitimate to allow fear to take you captive and control your thoughts about the character of God. It is legitimate to think through situations and act cautiously as a result.

I have no doubt that a victim of sexual abuse might be reading these words right now. There is someone, some sister or brother in Christ, who, like me, might be struggling with fear or anxiety. And many are struggling alone. No one knows.

If you are a victim, Christ's blood washes away shame. Abuse victims who may feel a sense of dirtiness can experience the real power of knowing they are white as snow before the Lord (Isaiah 1:18). We worship the God who draws near to the suffering and embraces the brokenhearted. There is no better news for a suffering brother or sister than the good news that Jesus Christ walked this earth perfectly; hung on a cross, bearing the full weight of shame, sin, and wrath on His back; and defeated death, rising from the grave. Jesus is now—right now—seated on the throne at the right hand of the Father. He is interceding for you and for me (Romans 8:34). I simply can't move on without sharing the good news with those of you who may resonate with what I've been describing in this section. It's the best news you will ever hear.

Although healthy fear seems most applicable in that sort of situation, there are definitely other times when fear is legitimate. Think about Jesus on the way to His crucifixion. He knew He was about to suffer the death of a criminal and the worse possible punishment of separation from His Father and wrath on behalf of undeserving sinners. While praying on the Mount of Olives, Jesus pleaded with His Father to find another way and in agony began to sweat drops like blood (Luke 22:42–44).[2] Justin Taylor and Andreas J. Köstenberger share about the account in *The Final Days of Jesus:*

> It is now late in the night. Upon entering the garden, Jesus instructs his disciples to sit at a certain location while he goes farther on with his closest disciples: Peter, James, and John. The time for discussion and instruction is now over, and Jesus is filled with sorrow and distress in anticipation of the coming events. He shares his anguish with his closest human friends: "My soul is very sorrowful, even to death; remain here, and watch with me" (Matt. 26:38).

Jesus' divinity did not eclipse his humanity (see John 11:35), and he keenly felt his need for human support and companionship during his final hours—it is no sign of weakness to want companionship and support before the evil face of death.

Going a little farther (a "stone's throw" according to Luke 22:41), Jesus engages in fervent personal prayer, crying out to his Father and imploring him to find another way—if there could be another way—yet ultimately submitting to God's will: "Abba, Father, all things are possible for you. Remove this cup from me. Yet not what I will, but what you will" (Mark 14:36). Jesus knows he is about to bear God's judgment for sin as a substitutionary sacrifice for the sins of the world. "Cup" was a common metaphor for God's righteous wrath poured out on sinners. Jesus is about to drink this "cup" in the place of others; he is the only one who could.[3]

Jesus was not cheering and jumping for joy as He faced the darkest time of His short life. He was rightly sorrowful. He knew that He was about to endure something miserable. Yes, it was worth it, and He knew that He would soon be with His Father, but during those moments in the garden we get a glimpse of Christ's humanity. He was emotionally drained; He was in agony. Jesus did not sin in His sorrow and distress—the reality of enduring suffering produced a natural emotion.

There are times when we might experience a similar emotion. No, it doesn't compare to what Jesus must have experienced, because for us who have trusted Jesus for our salvation, we know that upon death we will not experience wrath. But the sting of death is real. I imagine that the anticipation of a plane crash or knowing you are about to hit another car in an accident produces similar anguish. Knowing of the future grace we'll experience, we might not sinfully fear death, but it doesn't take away from the immediate emotion brought on by facing it.

With that said, there are times when we will experience the need to exercise a healthy fear. We want to be aware of our surroundings and be cautious. We want to trust the Lord, but trusting God doesn't call for foolishness or reckless abandonment. So telling your daughter not to speak with strangers isn't to instill the fear of men; it's to teach proper caution and wisdom. Asking a trusted male friend to walk you to your car at night isn't being silly; it's being smart. I fight, like many other women do, for faith and trust in God, who is my Father. He is the only one who knows the beginning and the end. He is the only Alpha and Omega. I can trust Him.

"But I have trusted in your steadfast love; my heart shall rejoice in your salvation. I will sing to the LORD, because he has dealt bountifully with me" (Psalm 13:5–6).

Chapter 5

FEAR OF NOT MEASURING UP

I jumped up like someone who had just been stung by a bee. I leapt from the bed, disoriented and fuzzy from a lack of sleep the night before. Kids do that. They have a way of sucking up the hours in the night that are designated for snoozing. I was late. I had to get my son dressed and to school, pack a lunch, and be prepared for a Skype meeting. (Why do people feel the need to meet "in person"? Video meetings with a toddler present are humorous at best, completely disastrous at worse. But I digress.) I had an hour to complete these tasks. I rolled out of bed, shook my son to get up and get ready, prayed we had Pop-Tarts so he would eat breakfast, pulled together "lunch" (maybe a few crackers, a cheese stick, and an orange), grabbed his little sister, and ran out the door. We made it! Everyone was alive. But something in my spirit just wasn't right. I felt like a failure.

It's not as if I'd set out to wake up late. I wasn't being lazy or idle. What if I had arisen with sufficient time to get into the Word and pray, wake up my child peacefully rather than in a fury of hurriedness, make a lunch that included all the basic food groups, get dressed, make a breakfast that wasn't out of aluminum packaging, and get back home in time for a peaceful meeting? Would I have felt better about myself? You betcha! I know I would have felt that I'd achieved. I know I would have felt that I'd had a nice, calm morning. I might also have attributed every bit of it to *me*.

But that morning was different. I woke up and realized that my red cape was missing. *Who stole it?* I thought. *Wait, someone took my power to get all things done in a single day too!* It's a shame, but I'm not Superwoman. And neither are you. We know this. We know that we are limited. We know that we can only do so much each day, and yet we strive and put pressure on ourselves to do more. Why? I think we fear not measuring up. There are so many rules that we try to keep up with. These rules include measuring up to our own standards, invisible standards, the world's standards, the church's potential standards, husband's standards, kids' standards—the list could go on and on.

In this chapter I'm going to dive into some of the ways in which we may fear we are failing miserably or just not measuring up. This is not an exhaustive list, but it includes some of the prominent ways that I've heard from other women or have personally experienced. And getting things done isn't the only pressure point placed on a woman, but it's the primary one I will address.

Getting Things Done

I imagine you can probably relate to my story about a rushed morning. I don't know what it is about our schedules, but how quickly do they become out of control? We are ruled by Google calendar, alarm clocks, planners, to-do lists. It is a never-ending cycle of running from place to place, a meeting with so-and-so, go, go, go. And if you don't relate to meetings and deadlines, maybe your list includes change the diaper, clean the floor, pickup from school, drive to ballet, and attend yet another baseball game. The list could go on and on. These tasks are all good things. Nothing about the activities and definitely not the people I listed are bad. As a matter of fact, they are gifts from God. Kids are a gift from the Lord. Work is a gift from the Lord. Church and fellowship are gifts from the Lord. But when we allow these things to rule us and then respond sinfully in anxiety, guilt, fear, or complaining, we need to evaluate where the source of the sin is coming from and probably take a good, hard look at our schedules.

We know that there are only twenty-four hours allotted in the day for work, sleep, eating, and play. And for the mom, in those allotted hours we must also find time to teach, admonish, play with, and nurture children. God is the only one not limited by time. He is eternal and self-existing, needing neither rest nor food. But in contrast, we are limited. We can be sick, depleted of energy, and tired fairly easily.

So instead of embracing our weakness and wisely resting or saying no, we try to cram as much as possible into one day. Maybe you are aware of your limitations but carry guilt on your shoulders. You may feel guilty because you can't find the energy to run around the house with your lively and active kids. You may feel guilty because your kids needed to watch yet another PBS show to enable you to finish a project. You may feel guilty because you have to say no to a project that you really desire to do. There are a number of pressures you face, and, besides anxiety, one thing that isn't often addressed is the temptation to feel guilty when you fear you are not going to get it all done. Later I'll share with you why you no longer have to succumb to guilt when you can't do it all.

A Lesson from the Littles

Sometimes I wonder if I'm teaching my kids, or if my children are teaching me. Sure, I am teaching them the ways of the Lord. I am teaching them to obey and submit. I am prayerfully teaching them to love their neighbor. And most importantly I try to demonstrate my own love for God and dependence on Him. But often it is because of them that I am reminded of various promises in Scripture or certain virtues. Recently I've been learning patience and stillness, the opposite of the rush and hurry that grips me at times.

My kids aren't in a hurry—ever. I, on the other hand, remain in a constant state of hurry. That might be an exaggeration, but, really, I'm in a hurry often. Yet because of my kids, I've been learning lately to slow down, soak in, and enjoy the here and the now. I so vividly saw my desire to hurry and my kids' eagerness to enjoy and explore life once when I was picking up my son from school. Just as we walked outside—my son on one side of me, holding his backpack, and my daughter on the other—they spotted a snail.

My kids were ecstatic and intrigued. They wanted to

look at it and pick it up and explore. They truly marveled at the creature—God's little creature. So I stopped too. My first thought was to hurry it along so we could get home, but I didn't. I let them watch the snail and enjoy the moment for as long as they wanted. After about ten minutes, they were done, so we moved on. It was so much fun to watch them. The kids had my undivided attention, and we both enjoyed the beauty of God's creation together. Moments like these go away—quickly! Kids grow up fast, and, as it does with us, the awesome wonder they experience during everyday life will fade. It was good for me to stop and enjoy one of these fleeting days and remember the Lord with my children.

So, why the hurry?

Rush, Rush, Rush for Nothing

When I stop to think about it, rarely do I have anything of much importance to be in a hurry for. But everything always seems so urgent. Perhaps it's the day and age we live in. The age of instant news, instant emails, instant connections—the age of the Internet. I could blame it on that, and I think it's fair to say that this age doesn't help my struggle, but really, it's just my heart.

I think that what I have to do is much more important than it really is. I'm a mini god during those times. My time is of great value even when I don't really have anything to do. Rushing and hurriedness produce anxiety, irritability, and impatience in my heart.

In Kevin DeYoung's book *Crazy Busy*, he describes the various dangers of being busy. One danger he wrote about that caused me to pause is that busyness can rob us of joy.

Instead of enjoying the wonderful gifts of children, a home, a husband, and even health, I can be scurrying around trying to take care of them all. DeYoung notes, "As Christians, our lives should be marked by joy (Phil. 4:4), taste like joy (Gal. 5:22), and be filled with the fullness of joy (John 15:11). Busyness attacks all of that. . . . When our lives are frantic and frenzied, we are more prone to anxiety, resentment, impatience, and irritability."[1]

Boy, do I get that. When I am busy, overextended, or not recognizing my limitations, I can become joyless. Have you ever snapped at your kids not because they misbehaved but just because you were trying to make dinner and maybe answer that email that seemed oh so important at the time— all at the same time? I have. The kid hadn't done anything wrong; I simply was trying to do too much all at once, got impatient and irritable, and allowed my tongue and sin to get the best of me. My joy was robbed, my child was hurt, and I felt remorseful—all for an email. Not worth it.

I want to put off those things, and the good news is that I *can*.

Trading Hurry for Peace

I'm learning to be set free from a selfish, self-focused, hurried life because Christ has set me free (Galatians 5:1). Even in situations where I struggle to slow down, like watching my kids look at snails, I'm learning to walk by the Spirit and not by the desires of my flesh. Let me tell you, the Spirit is much sweeter. In the simple act of stopping for my children, I was putting on love, joy, patience, kindness, gentleness, goodness, faithfulness, and self-control (Galatians 5:22–23). I'm so thankful that God would teach me and show me my sin so that I might change! As I am learning to slow down, I'm also learning to enjoy where I am. Only God can help me put off the temptation to hurry, and He is being faithful to do it.

Slowing down and putting off my old self is ultimately producing peace in my life. God is giving me peace in my heart about my supposed must-do's, peace while I wait, and peace to enjoy friends and family.

———— ✦ ————

If you fear you won't measure up because there's just so much that needs to be done and you simply can't do it all, leaving you feeling guilty and depleted, some of the best news you and I can hear is that we actually *cannot* do it all. The problem with guilt is that it condemns us and leaves us weary and without hope. Guilt says that the finished work on the cross was not enough, so we must bear our burden alone. In many ways, guilt is a self-centered focus on our limitations. It isn't a crime to be tired—it's a reminder of our need for God. It is a reminder of our need for a Savior. Guilt produces grief and sorrow and, in the end, spiritual death. You don't need to feel guilty for needing to rest. You just have to do it—rest. You don't need to feel guilty when saying no. You need to know that this is not failure.

I did a quick search on the Internet for "failure is not an option" and found that there are books written to help us make sure we embrace this concept. We don't want to fail. We want to do all things and do them well. I believe this is what plagues us. It isn't that we fear we will disappoint everyone we know; it's that ultimately we don't want to disappoint ourselves. We don't want to fail.

We want to be the best friend, the best neighbor, the best roommate, the best wife, the best mother, etc. There is an element of this desire not to fail that can be God-glorifying. God's Word tells us that whether we eat or drink, whatever we do, do it all for His glory (1 Corinthians 10:31). That means that we want to honor God in all our relationships—with friends, family, roommates, and neighbors. But, like Paul, as we desire to do good, evil is right there with us (Romans 7:21). The evil in this case is sin, and the sin that we struggle with when we desire not to fail for our own sake could be pride. Perhaps one way to fight our pride and embrace our weakness so that we can lean on Christ is to evaluate the ground we've been standing on.

Standing on Solid Ground

What if you are in a season in which rest is like a rare jewel—it's there but hard to come by. I understand. As a mom to young children, for example, rest is almost elusive. My situation has gotten better because my kids are slightly older now and are sleeping on regular cycles. But I remember those crazy days of waking up every three hours to feed a baby, only to wake up at my "normal" hour to the needs of a toddler. It is hard to tell a baby to wait while you get a little rest. It doesn't happen. We must acknowledge that there are seasons like this and cling to Christ. I hope the remainder of this chapter will bring you encouragement as you stare your weakness in the face.

I want to ask you, weary friend: What ground have you

been standing on? Many Sundays I proclaim with a loud voice, "On Christ the solid rock I stand." It's the beginning of a chorus to a beautiful hymn that has been written and rewritten, but its central message remains: only on Christ can we place our hope; anywhere else will fail us. Often for me, and I assume for you as well, it's not until things begin to shift underfoot that I realize I've been standing on the wrong ground. It isn't until I'm exhausted from trying so hard to be and do that I realize I haven't been resting in Him.

Following are some grounds we might stand on.

The ground of me. When I grow weary in doing good, I often discover I've been operating in my own strength. God so kindly urges us to rest in Him. I am weak, and when I realize my weakness, rather than proudly trying harder, God gives me grace. His grace is sufficient for me (2 Corinthians 12:9–10). This means that when I can't get it all done in a day, I don't have to feel guilty. I don't need to muster up enough energy—I need to rest. I need to rest in Him even when I can't rest physically. And when I feel that He is nudging me to physically rest, I need to do it and embrace my weakness and dependence on Him.

The ground of them. When I am discouraged because of the busyness of life, I often discover that I've been running around to please others. At first glance it might be easy to place the blame on the person who needs our attention. But we are never called to be ruled by others. We are called to serve others but never to be ruled by them. Of course, we are indeed to submit to proper authorities. What I have in mind is sinfully trying to please others. And we can't blame other people when it happens. It is not their burden to bear.

We must ask God for wisdom and know when to say no. This people pleaser knows how hard this is. Saying no will, however, only serve you and the other person in the long run. The stability of my feet and my faith should never rest in men.

The ground of circumstances. When all is well in the world, my heart and flesh don't fail me. As with the example of getting it all done, I am content as a bird flying high when I feel that I've accomplished what I needed to. But when circumstances become rocky, so can my foundation. I am tempted to despair. And though I know the truth of God's sovereignty and His goodness, I simply choose, at times, to ignore it.

The problem with our measures and these grounds we stand on is that if we complete our tasks or fulfill our desire, we're left feeling satisfied and good about ourselves. But when we do not complete our tasks or fulfill our desires, we feel only condemnation and guilt. The danger comes when we make these earthly standards into God's standards for us. In reality, God's standards are much greater than ours and far more difficult to achieve. The fear of not measuring up, as already mentioned, may really be a fear of failure, which could be rooted in self-righteousness and pride. And none of us are immune to it.

And yet . . .

When our hearts fail us, God continues to be our strength; He teaches us and is patient (Psalm 73:26). God chose the weak and leaky vessel to shame the strong (1 Corinthians 1:27). When I am weak, then I am strong (2 Corinthians 12:10).

Those Scriptures build my faith because I know that God

is with me through my weakness, but it doesn't solve my standing problem. My feet must stand firmly, securely on the hope I have in the gospel. My hope is built on nothing less than Jesus' blood and righteousness. Otherwise, I continue to strive, I continue to place unhealthy and unfair expectations on others and myself, and I continue to hope in my circumstances.

Jesus reminds me that I could never do enough or be enough but that I am enough because of Him—because He is enough. Jesus reminds me that all have sinned and fall short of the glory of God, so I can have grace for others who demand my time and attention, and He will enable me to lovingly serve them. Jesus reminds me that I have a great inheritance, so while the ground (or my soul) can give way, He is still my hope and stay. As the hymn proclaims, "On Christ the solid rock I stand / all other ground is sinking sand. / All other ground is sinking sand. . . . / When all around my soul gives way, / he then is all my hope and stay." I tell my soul: *Stop standing on sinking sand, please!*

He Measures Up

It can be a hard realization, but, as I've shared in this chapter, you and I don't measure up, and our fearful pursuit of measuring up is in vain. It would be sad if that was it. No hope. No good news. Just, "It is what it is." Thankfully, our reality is much better. We don't measure up, but Jesus does. The good news is that Jesus died and fulfilled the law that was required of us. The sweet cure for our fear of failure is the gospel, which reminds us of our limitations and weakness and our need for a Savior. Jesus is everything you and

I can never be on this earth. All our weaknesses were taken upon Him and paid for on the cross. All our imperfections are perfect in the sight of God because of Jesus.

Do you believe this? You will never overcome the fear of not measuring up until you embrace the finished work of Jesus on the cross. You won't be able to walk out your faith with confidence in Jesus until you understand that He is your risen King and is interceding for you now. He is so for you. There is no better news than this. You do not measure up, but He does.

Chapter 6

FEAR OF PHYSICAL APPEARANCE

Ladies, have you had a child? Do you notice that some things have changed? That which was once firm may be a little softer; for some, there are marks that will forever remind them of the nine months of carrying life. And I don't care what anyone says: your hips never return to their original position. Even if you haven't had the joy of carrying a child, you don't have to live long to be bombarded by what the world believes is the ideal body image. There are even websites dedicated to obtaining the ideal body shape. There are facial measurements for what is considered beautiful. And then there's our own sinful craving for these often unrealistic but definitely worldly measures. If we don't hit them, we don't measure up. So we become fearful and strive for this beauty.

Let me tell you, I've seen it all and have experienced much of it as well. I was a part of the fitness industry off and on for nearly eight years. Each January fitness facilities are flooded with new members and new participants in group fitness classes (where you would have found me teaching classes). I've seen the fitness addict, the disordered eater, and the constant scale watcher. And I've been her. I've had seasons when, if I didn't get in the gym, I would become discontent and fearful that I wouldn't be able to fit into my clothing. As a young girl, I struggled with eating issues—I never had a diagnosed eating disorder, but I was overly concerned with what went into my mouth. And scales were an enemy in college.

Now, as a mom of two and a writer who spends more time sitting than I have my whole life, I've experienced some serious body changes. My fears have ranged from failing to be attractive to my husband to not being able to fit into my clothing. I've feared not "getting it back." When it comes to body image, I've had to fight a fear of not measuring up to the standards of the world and the standards that I had placed on myself.

Isn't it so true that often good things are turned bad because of our sinful hearts? In other words, exercise and a desire to be healthy and steward well the body God has given us are not bad. It is when these desires become idols and we begin to measure our worth and value against them that they turn into something bad. Caring for our bodies can be a way to honor God. God created us not to lay waste to our bodies through abuse but to use them for His glory and purposes. And though godliness is of supreme value, we know that physical training is of some value to the Lord. Paul helps us see the dichotomy when he writes, "For while bodily training is of some value, godliness is of value in every way, as it holds promise for the present life and also for the life to come" (1 Timothy 4:8).

So we can assume that it is okay to pursue exercise as a goal for healthy living and, most importantly, for godly living. Exercise provides strength for service, it can be restorative, and it can be rejuvenating. But the fact that there is a need for exercise at all is another reminder that we live in a fallen world with fallen bodies.

Our bodies droop and change and grow tired. We try every experimental drug and various forms of exercise to prolong or prevent the inevitable. Botox and plastic surgery and a lifetime of marathons cannot prevent our inevitable fate. Like Adam in the Bible, we are dust and will return to dust (Genesis 3:19). No amount of exercise can stop it.

Companies such as Dove that make beauty products have taken on these false ideals of beauty.[1] In their ads they reveal the secrets to Photoshop. The images of the perfectly proportioned woman (tall and skinny or super curvy—whatever is your ideal) are most likely snipped and tucked via a computer and a graphic designer. So we can relax, ladies. We don't need to try to measure up to these false ideals of beauty. We don't need to fear this.

And while there is nothing on this earth to desire for all eternity, in God's kindness He doesn't leave us alone in our disintegration. We know that in time He will make all things new, and what was once rife with disease and pain will rise into glory with Christ. Paul connects the fall and our resurrection for us when he writes, "For as in Adam all die, so also in Christ shall all be made alive. But each in his own order:

Christ the firstfruits, then at his coming those who belong to Christ" (1 Corinthians 15:22–23).

As if that weren't good news enough, Paul reminds us that not only will we be with Christ but also that we will be like Him: "Our citizenship is in heaven, and from it we await a Savior, the Lord Jesus Christ, who will transform our lowly body to be like his glorious body, by the power that enables him even to subject all things to himself" (Philippians 3:20–21).

Yes! God will make it new. He will transform our bodies, the ones we are pulling and tucking and starving and beating to try to make beautiful. Yes, He will make our bodies beautiful, pure, and glorious when He returns. Our bodies will never die again. And, most importantly, we will be without sin.

Our fallen and imperfect bodies are yet another way we can look to Christ. By His grace, we can take our eyes off ourselves and fix them squarely on Jesus. Our bodies are made for worship, and if the Lord has us live long enough, we may be left with bodies that are unable to do anything but worship.

Each ache and pain and droopy muscle that was once firm is another reminder that we have a Savior who is perfect in beauty, and He is coming to get us, to return us to our pre-fall state, and to raise us to a condition more glorious than we can imagine.

So you might be thinking, *But I want to be attractive for my husband or future spouse.* If you resonate with this discussion about body issues, perhaps part of what motivates you to fear that you won't measure up to a certain man-made body image is a fear of not being desirable to a man. If you are married, this man may be your husband; if you are single, you may fear that you won't attract a male. (We must remember that godliness is ultimately attractive. Beauty is vain and will fade away, and only the fear of the Lord will last.) There is absolutely no problem with a desire to be attractive to your husband, until it becomes an idol that controls you and leads to fear and anxiety. If you fear not attracting a man if you don't obtain a certain body type, pray that the Lord would give you a man who fears the Lord above all else.

We don't want to live *for* man—for ourselves or for *a* man. The same weapon you use as you think through the issues of relationships is also used when fighting the temptation to strive for an ideal body. We must set our eyes above, on the Creator and realize that our bodies will never be ideal, and if they are, they won't always be while we are on this earth. Time will catch up to them eventually through death. This is the reality we all face.

Eating and the Ideal Body

There are several ways we women can struggle with body image, and while many were mentioned in passing above, one in particular seems to grip so many and in varying degrees that I think it's important not to breeze over it. Let's take a seat and face these really hard temptations together. Eating disorders are serious; many women are affected by them in some form (mild to severe) at some point. These disorders range from starvation, bulimia, and binge eating to milder forms of obsession over food intake. I am not addressing a general awareness of weight and diet, which is healthy and wise. We *should* take care of our bodies. What I'm addressing here is any temptation or action that consumes us and makes us think or do things that are harmful, unhealthy, or sinful. This is important to address also because, according to the National Institute of Mental Health, the severest cases of eating disorders are also the leading cause of death among women ages fifteen to twenty-four.[2] I know there are women who struggle deeply with the issue of eating disorders, many of which go undiagnosed. Others suffer milder forms that don't necessarily qualify as eating disorders but are still harmful and therefore important to include here.

During my senior year of high school, I hoped that I would continue my dancing and cheerleading once I got to college. The Lord had other plans, but it didn't stop me from experimenting with making myself throw up, crash diets, and constant mirror watching. I wanted to be able to make the team, and as a member of a competitive cheerleading squad in high school, I knew that the competition wasn't only in talent; it was also in weight. My freshman year of college was spent like much of my senior year in high school. I didn't make the college team, but I continued to teach cheerleading camps throughout the US on college campuses. After my sophomore year of college, I hung up my dancing and cheering days and was able to joyfully experience a freedom from striving for the perfect body.

I was never diagnosed with an eating disorder. I don't believe I had one. There wasn't much consistency to my struggle with food and weight. I was caught up in it at times and then was fine for months on end. My struggle was mostly rooted in acceptance. I wanted to fit the mold, make the team. Once I let go of that, I was able to move on from the desire to be skinny, but the sinful desire for acceptance continued to linger in my heart. I was no longer fixated on being skinny, but because I feared man, I continued to be disappointed that I could never be part of the team. As I addressed earlier, in the chapter on the fear of man, my heart found something else on which to set my desire for acceptance, which was simply to *be* accepted. God does and continues to root out the desire to please and be accepted by others.

The sort of fear and struggle I have in mind is commonly exposed by our eating habits. We don't necessarily all have eating disorders, but most of us likely have seasons of obsessive awareness of our bodies and/or what we eat. As I've reflected on that time in my own life, I think that what I experienced was an intensified version of many people's struggle. But I do have friends who have experienced eating disorders, and you might be reading this after having struggled or are even currently battling a disorder. Because of this, I've asked two friends to share their stories in their words. Their stories may not line up perfectly with your experience, but I do pray that they provide hope. The stories are merely excerpted here, but you can read them in their entirety in the appendix "Eating Disorders."

Eva's Story: Anorexia and the Mercy of God

I was saved at a young age, grew up in a Christian family, and was involved in a great church. I believed in God, prayed, sang songs, and sought to obey and please Him. However, despite being taught, I never grasped at a young age how deceitful and depraved my own heart was (and is!). I was a little legalist who knew the right answers and was proud of it. I remember distinctly standing in Walmart as a child, knowing that I wasn't supposed to look at the magazine racks by the register, but I thought I was mature enough to handle whatever was on them. I read a line saying, "Cheated on her . . . murdered," and thought, *I'm so glad I'm not that bad.* Grace wasn't amazing to me. Subconsciously, I thought sin had categories, and I just wasn't *that* bad. I really do believe I was a Christian as a child, but I was incredibly proud and self-righteous. I thought anorexia was stupid. "How could a girl starve herself?" I would ask.

As I grew outwardly (puberty, etc.), my craving for others' approval and self-righteousness also grew. I believed I could control my life, schedule, and appearance, and I looked down my nose at others who didn't have as much self-control. I was always active and thin growing up, but somewhere around fourteen or fifteen my approval-craving tendencies began to show me how much positive attention I received from being thin, athletic, disciplined, self-controlled, and toned. As my body changed in those teen years (hips happened), I began to work out regularly to stay in shape, but my activity was fueled by a desire to be praised and well thought of. The possibility of being overly obsessed never crossed my mind. (Read all of Eva's story in appendix 1.)

Emily's Story: An Open Letter to My Friends Struggling with Eating Disorders[3]

I want to take you back twenty years, to when I am thirteen years old.

I am a pastor's kid standing in a hospital room with clumps of hair in my hand.

My nails are splintered, and you can see the outline of my braces through my cheeks.

I weigh sixty pounds.

The room smells like Lysol. Nurses say I'm dying.

I was brushing my hair when it started to fall, and I tried to catch all the falling pieces and put them back on my head.

Today I ate for the first time in four years—truly ate, everything on my plate, everything they put before me— because even though I still don't think I have anorexia, I know this isn't normal.

To be purple from hypothermia and unable to run or lift objects, and to have your friends cry when they see you— this is not normal.

It will be another twenty years before I can admit to having a mental illness, but today is a start. Because I saw her on the way to the hospital. A woman, jogging, and she was muscular and the most beautiful woman I'd ever seen. She seemed fully alive.

And I realized, then, in that moment, that I was hungry for more than food.

I had been starving long before I ever refused my first meal.

I had no idea about anorexia nervosa. We were preacher's kids raised singing hymns and memorizing Scripture and homeschooled at our parents' long, wooden table. The only TV we watched was a black-and-white one we found at the dump. We pulled it up from the basement once a week for Sunday-night Disney. I wasn't allowed to take dance classes or look at fashion magazines because Mum, who was a nutritionist, thought they might trigger an eating disorder.

But darkness, like light, leaks in through the cracks.

And if we're forced to deny our sin from the day we're born, we'll never realize we need a Savior. We'll only ever punish ourselves for not being what we feel we're supposed to be: perfect.

I had only ever been a good girl, quiet unless spoken to. I took care of my younger siblings. I spent hours on my poems and my pictures, hoping to earn the attention of a father who spent most of his time at the church or in his office.

I was never asked what my favorite color was. I didn't know my favorite color until I was married, a seemingly small thing until you realize it's not just that—you also don't know how you like your eggs done, or your steak, or what your favorite shampoo is because all you know is that it has to be inexpensive.

It's the small things that eventually add up to become the big picture of why you don't love yourself.

And when I was thirteen and standing there in that green hospital gown, Mum telling me in her soft British accent that nurses said I was a miracle because I was still alive (I should have died), it felt like God reaching down and cupping my cheeks and saying, "I will never leave you nor forsake you."

It was my heavenly Father reassuring me there was more to life than rules and liturgies. There was joy—and it tasted good.

Friend, have you tasted that joy?

I finally knew, in spite of the pain of my childhood and the clumps of hair in my hand, that God loves me because He made me. And even more, because He died for me. And suddenly my body was no longer just skin covering muscle covering bone. It was a vessel, and God wanted to pour His love into me so I could pour it into others. We are not just physical beings. We are spiritual, and part of me always knew this, and this is why food was never enough.

But it took relapsing one more time into anorexia as a young married woman to not only acknowledge God's love for me but also let it fill me, because joy is not found in a perfect life. Joy is the peace that transcends all understanding as we look into the eyes of our Maker and see that we can trust Him in spite of the pain around us. God is trustworthy.

I used to think the famous miracle in John 6 was all about bread, fish, and five thousand empty stomachs that needed dinner. Yet I always found myself perplexed about why Jesus would allow such waste—why He'd create twelve baskets of leftovers.

But that's to miss the point. The story is not about bread or fish.

As Jesus later explained to the crowd, "I am the bread of life; whoever comes to me shall not hunger, and whoever believes in me shall never thirst" (John 6:35).

Jesus is the bread. He is the eternal sustenance for the hungry soul. In Him our souls no longer go hungry or thirsty. The leftovers in the story are a picture for us, reminding us every time we read it that He is more than enough for you and more than enough for every need in my life.

To feed on living bread is to find Christ sufficient for every hunger pang I feel in my soul, to let His grace and goodness fill all the empty, aching places inside of me, to nourish and grow me strong in faith and love.

Friend, do you know this living bread? (Read all of Emily's story in appendix 1.)

These are their stories, and the Lord is writing your story. It may not be just like theirs; you may have experienced years and years of struggle and battle with little to no relief. There are a number of resources available to help you with the battle, and I urge you to seek help. But we can join with Milton Vincent and say:

So this is my story, ongoing it is.
How shall I thank God for this gospel of His?
A gift that keeps giving,
the gospel confers,
The bounty of heaven each time I rehearse.[4]

Chapter 7

FEAR OF SEXUAL INTIMACY

I've been married for eleven years. Eleven years for some seems like forever and for others like just a beginning. In our short (or long?) years of married life I have struggled off and on with a fear of not measuring up to the ideal wife. You know what wife I'm thinking of. The one who is "far more precious than jewels." This woman apparently wakes up super early—it's still dark outside, and she has already taken care of her children. She's business savvy and also sews clothing. Who does both? Well, apparently she does. She is generous to the poor and caring. The woman is careful with her time; she will have nothing to do with idleness. If you haven't already guessed, I'm writing about the Proverbs 31 woman. This beautiful character in Scripture is not intended to be a mandate or to pressure women. But how often have we gone to this list of virtues and despaired or lamented? *She does good and not harm to her husband all his life?* we think.

Well, I've failed. I was sinfully angry just yesterday.

My first year of marriage was a mixture of trying to be this perfect wife and trying to change my husband. I struggled greatly with self-righteousness. I wanted us to fit a certain mold. I had a fear of not measuring up to this ideal—you know, the "godly couple." My fear mounted that we wouldn't be good, godly examples, while I was also judging my husband almost relentlessly.

And I know I'm not alone in this temptation.

I've spoken to newly married girlfriends who have told me of their frustrations with their new spouse. There is generally some area in which these women wish their husbands would improve, and they are growing weary waiting. While their husbands may need to grow, it's easy and common for the wives to struggle with being judgmental and self-righteous. We can look at our men, see sin, and be too quick and eager to point it out. Worse, we can look at them and not see the grace so evident in their lives and our own sinfulness.

I relate. That was me.

I remember my wedding like it was yesterday. It was a cold yet beautiful December day. All of our decorations were red, white, and green to reflect the season. It was exactly what we hoped it would be and more.

After the honeymoon (which was all but magical), we returned to our home eager to start our new lives together as one. But soon the fairy tale ended, and real life began. It didn't look quite like I had imagined. There were no glaring problems. No deep-rooted sin issues. Yet I was extremely aware of my husband's shortcomings, and I wasn't holding back on sharing my thoughts.

I was quick to point out sin and eager to share "observations" about how he could change or grow as a leader, all under the pretense of being his helper. I judged my husband harshly our first year of marriage. I thought I was right, and I played the role of his "holy spirit." Like I said, I masked it as being his helper. Wrong!

But wasn't I helping him by sharing my wisdom and insights into every single part of his life? I mean, surely he needed my help to become a godly man, right? Let's just say that there was a plank in my eye the size of a California redwood, but all I could see was the speck in his (Matthew 7:3). I was filled with self-righteousness and self-absorption.

Behind all this nagging was a desire to have it all together. Also, so much of my corrections stemmed from a desire to fill some perceived need of mine and had little to do with his sanctification. My desire was that he would change for *me*, not to please and glorify God. My observations were generally (though not always) selfish.

As I mentioned, I'm so very thankful the Lord has given my husband and me more years to grow. Now, eleven years after our wedding day, I'm still learning how to lovingly help my husband, but even more I am learning how to *enjoy* him. I've learned that God has designed us both for a purpose, and we do not need to live up to the standards we set for ourselves or the pressures we think we may experience from outside of us. I have grown in looking for areas of grace and for gifts. God has helped me use my tongue to encourage, build up, and praise my husband for how God has made him rather than to tear him down for how God *didn't* make him.

And just as I'm not surprised by my sin, I'm equally

unsurprised that God would help me grow in this area. God works all things together for the good of those who love Him (Romans 8:28). He provides a way of escape for our sinful self-righteousness (1 Corinthians 10:13). He promises to finish the good work He began in you and in me (Philippians 1:6). This is good news for us! God is faithful.

Amazingly, even when I fell into the temptation to judge my husband and attempted to meet the perceived standards of those around me, God remained unswervingly committed to forgiving me, because my sin—not in part but the whole— is covered in the blood of Jesus Christ. And, sister, so is yours.

---◆---

My self-righteousness was rooted in pride and the fear of man. But fearing that we wouldn't be an awesome and super-human couple wasn't my only battle. I also was concerned that I would disappoint *him*. During our first year of marriage (again, so thankful for years *after* the first one), I did truly comical things, like make dessert after *every* meal. It didn't help the body-image struggle. I was only a mediocre house cleaner and would be so discouraged thinking that I had dis-appointed my husband when the house wasn't as clean as I thought he desired (he never once pressured me to do any of this, honestly). So if those weren't really his standards, and the Lord wasn't demanding them of me, where was the pressure coming from? I had adopted the culture around me. I was not alone in these pursuits to be the perfect wife. The only prob-lem was, it wasn't possible. I was chasing after wind.

As I have been involved in various women's ministry

events, I realize this remains a temptation for many of us. We pressure ourselves to be the ideal that we hope will please our husband, but in reality those pursuits are self-absorbed and prideful. God is a God of order, and therefore there is nothing at all wrong with a desire for a home that reflects that order. Titus 2 encourages older women to teach younger women to be busy at home, so, again, paying attention to our homes is good and important. But when we place pressure on ourselves, and we pursue being an "excellent wife" out of fear, it does not please the Lord.

We are going to come back to the Proverbs 31 woman, because we do have something to learn from her besides the practical application of being a wife and mother. The woman was a great example, but maybe not for the reason you think.

Intimacy with Him

I'm not going to go in-depth on the topic of intimacy. There's so much that could be written, so much that it could fill its own book. But it would behoove me to note this struggle that many women experience when thinking about intimacy. You may wonder or worry: *Will I measure up? Will I be enough for my husband?*

This temptation seems most prevalent in new brides. You've just walked down the aisle with the man you've been waiting for—and if you've waited for *that* day, it can seem scary and intimidating. As I've interacted with new brides, most seem concerned and worried with thoughts like, *What if I don't know what to do? How in the world will I be able to be naked and unashamed?* Philippians 4:8–9 could prove to be a helpful guard as you enter the bedroom. Think true thoughts about your husband and don't place undue pressure on yourself to perform. You have a lifetime to get it right! Pressure's off. Enjoy it. Enjoy him. And if you need help figuring it all out, be open and honest with your husband, or ask a trusted older woman for advice, or both.

But the truth is, it's not always so smooth, and there are other struggles that we will explore.

I Wore White

It was a beautiful, simple, bell-cut dress with delicate lace. We printed our testimony in the program as a reminder of all God had done to bring us to this pinnacle point—marriage. My white wedding dress was a visible reminder to me that I was pure, white as snow, and forgiven before the Lord. I was walking toward my future husband clothed in Christ's righteousness and aware of the deep and meaningful oneness that the night would bring.

My white dress did not represent a life of purity. It did not represent a young, blushing bride who had waited to know the mysteries of the intimacy reserved for the bride and groom. My white dress did not represent a born-again virgin. Rather, it represented a born-again Christian (John 3:1–15). God sought me, saved me, and made me a new creation and has given me a living hope (1 Peter 1:3).

And yet even today I can long for a different testimony. I can look at my past indiscretions and feel shame. This has never been heaped upon me by my loving husband, so why the struggle?

I think, in part, it could be that I do understand the seriousness of sexual immorality. The Scriptures warn that the sexually immoral do not have a place in the kingdom of God (Ephesians 5:5). Matthew says that if a man even looks with lustful eyes, he's committed adultery (Matthew 5:28). Even Paul, a man called to celibacy, instructs the Corinthians not to withhold sex in the confines of marriage—temptation to sexual immorality is too great (1 Corinthians 7:1–5).

I am not defined by that old, raggedy sin. I don't need to walk in fear and shame. I've been accepted by my husband and, most importantly, by my Lord.

But I think there's more to the shame that I experience creeping up in my gut. It often comes after I've read an article or a post warning this generation of the seriousness of sexual sin. I agree with much of what I read, but then at some point I find myself being told that I won't be able to fully love my husband or that a woman doesn't lust. My head begins to burn as this coal sits and sinks down into my skull (Romans 12:20). It's hard to be a woman with a sinful past, especially one of an impure nature. We are expected to be pure and undefiled. And most temptations to sexual sin are attributed to men. So not only are we sinful; we are also quite abnormal (at least by appearances). We are no longer even women—we are man-like.

Paul helps us again in his address to the Corinthians: "No temptation has overtaken you that is not common to man" (1 Corinthians 10:13a). Temptation to sexual sin is not isolated to men. Jesus knows this to be true. As He walked the earth, He interacted with prostitutes, He challenged the adulterer, and then He died for them—and for you and me.

Here's more good news: "God is faithful, and he will not let you be tempted beyond your ability, but with the temptation he will also provide the way of escape, that you may be able to endure it" (1 Corinthians 10:13b). Even now you find yourself battling daily the temptation to sexual sin. There is a way of escape. You can say no to sin. You don't have to fall into sexual sin. If you have God's Spirit, you have the power to turn and run in the other direction.

If you struggle with the shame of *forgiven* sin but have placed your hope in the finished—oh, thank You, Lord, that it is finished—work of Christ, then you don't have to fear punishment. You don't have to walk in shame. You don't have to long for a different testimony as if God didn't say, "For *all* have sinned and fall short of the glory of God" (Romans 3:23). Christ took it all on Him the moment He hung on that cross. You don't have to suffer your own punishment—He did for you.

I wore white on my wedding day, and I'd wear it again. I am a new creation. The old is gone. That doesn't mean I'm without temptation, but I am not defined by that old, raggedy sin. I am not defined by my past. I am born again—a Christian.

And you don't have to fear what your future spouse will think of you. Pray that God would bring you a man who is so in love with Jesus and so in love with grace that he would be able to see you as God does, clothed in Christ's righteousness. Pray that your future spouse would know the Word and what God says about sin, justification, and grace. And then believe that the Lord, who is faithful, will take care of the rest.

If your husband continues to struggle with your past sexual history, it might be wise to seek the help of a pastor or counselor who can assist you and your marriage.

Walking through the struggles with intimacy can feel lonely. My friend shares her story below in hope of encouraging your faith and as a reminder that there are many who are working through this.

One (Anonymous) Girl's Struggle with Intimacy and God's Continued Help

I was terrified about my wedding night. I was very attracted to my fiancé, so you would think that I would have been nothing but excited; however, I knew my guy had a dark past in pornography. Although God had pulled him out of that lifestyle, I wasn't naïve to the fact that his expectations about what women were like in the bedroom were unknowingly shaped by what he had viewed in the past. I was gripped with fear that I wouldn't live up to these other women and that he would be so disappointed or even bored. It wasn't so much that I was afraid for him to see me naked (although that was scary too) as it was that I feared what he thought of my performance, so to speak. Although we had a blast on our honeymoon, there was also a lot of stress because of these surrounding issues. I have more clarity to speak about things now, but initially we didn't have any helpful conversations about it because I didn't fully understand the complexities. All I knew was that I was really scared.

As I look back on this, I think there were a few things going on. My past, which would sound tame to anyone who has lived a worldly life, might have hindered me. I had many boyfriends as a preteen and on into college. There was one in high school whom I stuck with a bit longer than the others. In that relationship, I walked the tightrope of virginity and only technically crossed to the other side still a virgin. Our physical involvement was pretty much the only component to our relationship. I remember wanting to make him happy but not wanting to do any of the things he wanted me to do. I would push him away but eventually give in. I felt so guilty but continued on in the relationship until the Lord used a friend to challenge me, which gave me the courage to end things.

I have carried many memories from that relationship into my marriage. I feel restrained in some ways, because those memories bring back a sick feeling of the past with that other guy. I wonder if this all plays into my fear of not pleasing my husband and having to do things I don't want to do in order to please. My husband is different in every way from that old boyfriend, but sometimes even irrational fears with no basis in reality can surface.

The second thing that may have contributed to my fear is the way I was raised. My family is a wonderful, authentic, Christian family. One thing we never talked about, however, was sex. It was simply too awkward. I wonder if I would have had the courage to talk to my parents about what was going on with my boyfriend if we'd been having ongoing conversations about sexuality. I eventually ended that un-healthy relationship with my boyfriend through the encouragement of friends, but my parents never knew all that had happened. Then, as a married adult, I still found it awkward to talk about sex, even with my husband.

And, lastly, my fear of man caused me to fear. I feared what my husband thought of me sexually more than I actually wanted to please him or enjoy intimacy with him. I was like the junior-high kid who cannot bring herself to step out and dance because she wrongly assumes everyone is staring at her to make fun of every wrong move.

Today, I don't think I have fully overcome my fears. I have come a long way though. I feel that my husband and I made a huge breakthrough when it dawned on us how much the relationship with my high school boyfriend had impacted me. My husband had struggled with frustration through the first five years of our marriage because I was so nervous, hesitant, and reserved sexually. The only conclusion he could come to was that I wasn't attracted to him, which wasn't the case. When we realized some of the cause of my issues, he was motivated and strengthened to have patience with me. His patience and lack of tension, over time, helped me to relax and focus on him. It also helped me to remind myself that he is a completely different guy from the ghost of my past and that I can make new memories with my husband. I have also prayed about these things. I haven't seen an immediate change but have continued to ask God for help anyway. Looking back, I can see a huge improvement in our intimacy.

Pornography in Marriage

Earlier I shared how women can be fearful that they won't measure up in the bedroom simply because they are virgins, and the thought of jumping from zero to one hundred on their wedding night seems daunting. This temptation to fear not measuring up in the bedroom is common, but today many women may have competition in this area that they never imagined they'd have to battle. No, it's not another woman in the flesh; instead it is pixilated images that appear on the screen, robbing many men of the joy of real intimacy and pleasure. It's pornography, and it is another cause of this anxiety within women. The onslaught of pornography and the unfortunate temptation and stronghold it has on men (and women) is staggering. I'll be honest: I find it difficult to fully wrap my head around the sheer number of people who not only struggle with pornography but also are ensnared in it. There are forty million regular users of pornography in the United States.[1] As I sit and type, I have to pause, cover my mouth, and hold back tears. One writer has dubbed it the "new narcotic."[2] Scientists have determined a number of reasons for this addiction—primarily that arousal is addictive.[3] We are also aware that this unfortunate epidemic has wreaked havoc on marriages. Men are struggling to become aroused with their wife, and wives are left feeling deflated and confused.

If you've decided you can't compete with pornography, good—you are right. No one can compete with a completely false scenario. Nothing about what is performed is the reality (or the potential joy) of real intimacy. So what is a woman to do when she fears that she won't measure up to her husband's needs because of the proliferation of pornography? Following are a few thoughts.

Think true thoughts. As I mentioned earlier, Philippians 4:8–9 serves us in many ways and circumstances. Unless your husband has confessed being tempted by pornography, don't assume he will have this struggle. The last thing you should do is read this chapter and then assume that your man is among the many. There are indeed men who *do not* struggle with pornography use.

Seek counsel. If you've discovered that your husband is having trouble with intimacy because he has a porn habit, a good option might be to seek counsel from a faithful pastor who can help direct you where to go next. There is no doubt that you have experienced great loss—loss of trust, loss of faith, loss of hope. In her book *When Your Husband Is Addicted to Pornography*, Vickie Tiede shares her story of betrayal and hope. Through her personal experience she reminds the reader, "It doesn't matter if you've experienced small losses or tremendous ones; they are real and significant in your life. Face them and allow yourself to feel the heartache, knowing that there is One who understands and feels your pain."[4] You don't have to grieve alone.

Remember God. In all our talk about fear, our only true rescue from it all is to remember God. God has the power to free your husband from this temptation, and God has the power to renew in you fresh faith for intimacy. He can do that. Pastor John Piper offers a bit of hope:

> Moreover, we know from experience that we are not slaves of these powerful pornographic changes in our brains. I do not minimize them. Judging by the ongoing effects, even in my sixties, of my teenage tomfoolery, I have tasted the amazing staying power of old sinful patterns. But we are not horses or mules that can only be curbed with bit and bridle (Psalm 32:9).[5]

Remember, God is able to do more than we could ever imagine.

Chapter 8

WHY WE CAN TRUST GOD

Have you ever been told to trust the Lord? I know I have. I've been told that a lot, actually. And I know that I've said the same to others as well. It's easy to toss around phrases such as "Trust God," but why should we? The name of this book is *Fear and Faith*. We've discussed unpacking our fear. There is no doubt we all fear in one area or another (many, like me, probably in several areas). But I want to turn our attention now to the One who provides the help we need not only to face our fears but also to rest in the midst of them. Rest may first require repentance and then trust, but before we can get there, we need to know why we can trust God. So we turn our attention now to Him. In order for us to have faith to trust God, we need to know who He is. Part of the faith we hope to obtain comes from fearing the Lord. I am going to explain in chapter 9 what it means to fear the Lord, but let's go ahead and define a few terms to help us get started.

Solomon begins the book of wisdom with a peculiar statement: "The fear of the LORD is the beginning of knowledge; fools despise wisdom and instruction" (Proverbs 1:7). This statement can sound to me like the chicken and the egg. What comes first: Knowledge? Wisdom? Fear of the Lord? How can you fear the Lord before you obtain knowledge? Is it possible to really know God and not fear Him? The definition of terms really does make a difference.

Knowledge refers to correct understanding of the world and oneself as creatures of the magnificent and loving God. Wisdom is the acquired skill of applying that knowledge rightly.[1] We want to *obtain* knowledge, which will give us a correct understanding of the world. And in the case of this book, we are gaining an understanding of who God is and His ways in light of our circumstances. So before we can fear the Lord (which we will jump into soon), we must know God, and knowing God means more than just knowing that there is a God. J. I. Packer explains: "How are we to do this? How can we turn knowledge *about* God into knowledge *of* God? The rule for doing this is simple but demanding. It is that we turn each truth that we learn about God into matter for meditation *before* God, leading to prayer and praise *to* God."[2]

In other words, to know God, we must meditate on the truth of God. God reveals Himself in His Word. It is there that we meet Him and know Him. Knowledge of God ultimately transforms the knowledge of all things. So we can look at stars and worship or learn about blood vessels and be in awe of the Creator. But we cannot rightly do any of this without first knowing God.

From the day my son was born, I would tell him that God

made the world and gave him to us. I had two miscarriages before my son was born, so I found myself constantly thanking God for him. As a baby, of course, my little guy couldn't really respond. But then, around the age of four, he finally shared his thoughts about God, which surprised me. He said, "I don't believe you. Where is He? I don't think God is real." See, my son also knew of dragons, superheroes, strange creatures with several heads, and Thomas the Tank Engine, who spoke to him through the television screen. He knew these weren't real; he knew they were characters. But they seemed so much more real to him because he *saw* them. What I realized then is that it would take the Lord imparting faith to my son for him to *believe* that God is real and not just some abstract, imaginary thing his mommy liked to speak about.

I think we can be like my son. We hear people talking about this God; we even might speak of Him ourselves. But do we actually know who He is? And, if we do, do we *believe* it in our hearts? James tells us that even the demons believe and shudder (James 2:19). Belief alone isn't what gives us the assurance that God is who He says He is. Even as born-again believers, we can never have enough knowledge of God. And let's be honest: during those terrifying moments of fear and dread, we so often forget. That's why it's good to be reminded of who God is.

What Is God?

The Westminster Shorter Catechism tells us that "God is Spirit, infinite, eternal, and unchangeable in his being, wisdom, power, holiness, justice, goodness, and truth." God is so great, so magnificent, so awesome in everything He is and does. As

Packer so eloquently wrote, "Like us, he is personal; but unlike us, he is *great*."[3] There have been books upon books written about the character and attributes of God. What I write here won't be exhaustive. Is there any way to truly exhaust our understanding of God? This won't come close. I'm not going to attempt to address every aspect of our Father (His fatherhood being yet another attribute); instead I am going to share those characteristics about Him that I think will aid us in the chapters ahead. Those characteristics include but are not limited to His sovereignty, wisdom, love, and goodness.

But before we can move to those characteristics, we must agree that God is not like us. God is holy, or set apart. He is completely pure. He is completely other than anything our finite minds can imagine, and though we are made in His image, He is nothing like us (we can be like Him, but He is not like us). In the song of Moses we read, "Who is like you, O LORD, among the gods? Who is like you, majestic in holiness, awesome in glorious deeds, doing wonders?" (Exodus 15:11). The answer is, there is no one like our God. God is glorious. God is magnificent. God is any adjective you can think of that describes something great. So often in our thinking, we minimize God by envisioning that He is like us. How we think of God is revealed in how we live and what we say and in the private meditations of our heart. God is more awesome than anything we could ever think. His holiness, to me, is the foundation for all aspects of His character.

The Sovereignty of God

> O house of Israel, can I not do with you as this potter has done? declares the LORD. Behold, like the clay in

the potter's hand, so are you in my hand, O house of Israel. (Jeremiah 18:6)

With God are wisdom and might; he has counsel and understanding. (Job 12:13)

Scripture pours forth great details about the sovereignty and wisdom of God. These are attributes that, for many, are hard to grasp. A. W. Tozer explains: "To say that God is sovereign is to say that He is supreme over all things, that there is no one above Him, that He is absolute Lord over creation."[4] There is no other being like God. As we understand that God is sovereignly ruling and reigning and that He is the only God, we can begin to relinquish our control. Our fear tells us we are in control, that we *need* to be in control and submit to our feelings. God's sovereignty reminds and reassures us that He is in control and that He is wise. His thoughts are not our thoughts, and His ways are not our ways. This is good news.

Timothy needed this news to fight the good fight of faith. Paul instructed Timothy to stay in Ephesus "that [he] may charge certain persons not to teach any different doctrine" (1 Timothy 1:3). Timothy was supposed to confront false teachers. Can you imagine for a minute that this would be your calling? Sure, we are all supposed to proclaim truth, and when we see or hear something false, to help correct it (Ephesians 4:15). But not many of us are *charged* with looking for and correcting false teachers in an entire city! The beauty of this calling for Timothy was that it was motivated by and had its aim in loving others (1 Timothy 1:5). Nevertheless, this was a weighty task, one that required great faith.

At the end of 1 Timothy, Paul doesn't tell Timothy he needs to man up, and he doesn't tell him to trust himself or that he can do it. Paul reminds Timothy of who God is. Timothy fights the good fight of faith by remembering that at the proper time, he will be with the one "who is the blessed and only Sovereign, the King of kings and Lord of lords, who alone has immortality, who dwells in unapproachable light, whom no one has ever seen or can see" (1 Timothy 6:15–16). When Timothy needed reassurance about sharing the truth, he was encouraged to remember that God is sovereign (ruling) over that moment and that he should trust that God will do as He pleases with what was shared. Most importantly, Timothy knew that those who opposed him were nothing compared to God. He could trust and lean on God. As can we.

> For his dominion is an everlasting dominion, and his kingdom endures from generation to generation; all the inhabitants of the earth are accounted as nothing, and he does according to his will among the host of heaven and among the inhabitants of the earth; and none can stay his hand or say to him, "What have you done?" (Daniel 4:34–35)

The Wisdom of God

And God, who is sovereign, *acts* through His wisdom. And guess what? He is *all*-wise.

The dictionary defines wisdom as "knowledge that is gained by having many experiences in life, the natural ability to understand things that most other people cannot understand, and knowledge of what is proper or reasonable: good sense or judgment."[5] That is a human understanding of wisdom. We become wise as we gain understanding. We make smart choices and therefore are wise. We gain experience and are able to discern what is good through experience and therefore act in ways that are wise. God, on the other hand, never had to be taught, never had to experience, never had to read and study. God is all-wise.

God is not only all-wise; He is also wise in all He does. Nothing is done by God apart from the wisdom of God. The psalmist sings, "O LORD, how manifold are your works! In wisdom have you made them all; the earth is full of your creatures" (Psalm 104:24). And we see in Romans that He is the only wise, the only completely and fully wise, God: "To the only wise God be glory forevermore" (Romans 16:27). Doesn't that blow your mind? God has always existed, and He does what He wills, and He does it all with complete wisdom. Mind blown! His wisdom means He knows what is best.

The old hymn "God Moves in a Mysterious Way" by William Cowper captures the wisdom of God well. In it Cowper declares the wisdom of God's ways, even through trouble. We won't fully understand His ways, and unbelief will scream lies into our ears about the character and wisdom of God, but in due time His great will shall be made known to us. And Cowper didn't write the hymn because he had great joy in the midst of his sorrows. Cowper suffered through depression, great doubt, and suicide attempts.[6] But his words live on through hymnals and worship services. Read the lyrics of his hymn:

O God, in a mysterious way
great wonders you perform.
You plant your footsteps in the sea
and ride upon the storm.
Deep in unfathomable mines
of never-failing skill,
you treasure up your bright designs
and work your sovereign will.

O fearful saints, fresh courage take.
The clouds you so much dread
are big with mercy and shall break
in blessings on your head.
Our unbelief is sure to err
and scan your work in vain.
You are your own interpreter,
and you will make it plain.[7]

In the midst of great trouble Job also declared the wisdom of God. We get a glimpse of Job's view of God when he says: "His wisdom is profound, his power is vast. Who has resisted him and come out unscathed?" (Job 9:4 NIV); and, "With God are wisdom and might; he has counsel and understanding" (Job 12:13).

If you remember the story of Job, then you know that he lost everything. And by "everything," I mean everything that was of any importance to him. Job lost *everything*. At the end of his story, as he repents and sings great praise to God, Job proclaims, "I know that you can do all things, and that no purpose of yours can be thwarted" (Job 42:2). Job suffered greatly, and, I imagine, he was very confused. His friends didn't do a good job of comforting him; Job even called them "miserable comforters" (Job 16:2). But Job turned to God and was convinced of the wisdom of God even in the midst of great pain and confusion.

And what did God do? He restored Job and his fortunes. He gave him twice as much livestock as he had previously possessed and gave him more children: seven sons and three daughters. Job was restored to his family and friends. The Lord worked in mysterious ways. The end of Job highlights to me the familiar passage of Romans 8. I think, in the end, Job knew a truth about God that hadn't even been uttered yet:

> What then shall we say to these things? If God is for us, who can be against us? He who did not spare his own Son but gave him up for us all, how will he not also with him graciously give us all things? Who shall bring any charge against God's elect? It is God who justifies. Who is to condemn? Christ Jesus is the one who died—more than that, who was raised—who is at the right hand of God, who indeed is interceding for us. Who shall separate us from the love of Christ? Shall tribulation, or distress, or persecution, or famine, or nakedness, or danger, or sword? (Romans 8:31–35)

God doesn't do anything in His sovereign will that isn't both wise and loving, which leads us to another attribute of God's—His love.

The Love of God

Here's more good news: We don't serve a God who is only sovereign and only wise. He is *also* infinitely loving. God's love is incomprehensible. We can't fathom it, and when we try to compare our love to God's love, we fall awfully short.

We've heard it said before that God is love. And though this is completely true, it has caused some confusion. You can't and shouldn't say that God is all love and no wrath, or that God is all wrath and no love. Everything He is and does is equal. There are many times when I find myself, as I read God's Word and think about His attributes, as I have done in these chapters, stopping and joining David to say, "Such knowledge is too wonderful for me; it is high; I cannot attain it" (Psalm 139:6). When thinking about God's love, I am often struck with awe. I'm amazed that His love was ultimately manifested in the death of His only Son, and I am amazed to know that in all He does, He is still loving. I'm most likely to compare my love to His, and my love falls wholly short. So what is the love of God, and how do we see it?

First, God loves all He has made. In the beginning He provided everything that we would need; He created it and said it was very good (Genesis 1:31). When Adam and Eve fell into sin (this didn't surprise God; He is all-knowing), He rightly punished them for their disobedience, but out of His great love, He covered them (Genesis 3:21), a foretaste of the covering that all those who believe receive through Christ. God takes care of even the birds of the air (Matthew 6:26). These are manifestations of the love of God. And as D. A. Carson puts it, "All the manifestations of the love of God emerge out of this deeper, more fundamental reality: love is bound up in the very nature of God. God is love."[8]

Let's explore that famous Scripture passage from which we get the description "God is love." In 1 John 4 there is a compelling call for Christians to love one another. John explains that love doesn't originate from us. If we love, it is because we have been "born of God" and "[know] God" (v. 7). And then John says, "Anyone who does not love does not know God, because God is love" (v. 8). God is love. All that we know about God is bound up one way or another in His love. He loves us with an everlasting love, a love that began before the foundation of the world (Psalm 103:17; Ephesians 1:4). As one commentary puts it, "God is love" means that God continually gives of Himself to others and seeks their benefit.[9] Every wise act in His mysterious sovereignty is an act of love.

We must understand this as we seek to make sense of our lives and to fully understand God. God gives us glimpses of His incredible love, and the greatest taste of it is through the blood of Christ. "In this is love, not that we have loved God but that he loved us and sent his Son to be the propitiation for our sins" (1 John 4:10). This is a love that we could never fully fathom. The gospel is where the Lord chooses to display His love in full. God loved the world and gave His Son to save the world (John 3:16). The gospel motivates us to trust God. We know that He is loving, and He has proven His great love through sending His perfect Son to die a sinner's death. During our times of fear, we can remember that we are loved and forgiven, and we can rest in Him.

The Goodness of God

Could it be said that if God is all-loving, then He must also be good? I think so. At the beginning of Psalm 107 the community sings out, "Oh give thanks to the LORD, for he is good, for his steadfast love endures forever!" (v. 1). Why are they giving thanks? They do so because His love endures forever. Why does His love endure forever? It endures because He is good. He is a good God—He can't separate His goodness from His love. As I've already written, love doesn't mean that we will get everything we desire and that we won't endure hardships. Often God's love looks nothing like what you and I would hope or expect, but we know that for those who love God, all things work together for good, for those called for a purpose (Romans 8:28). What He does is good and works for the good of others. God even assures us that He finishes the good work He began because He is good and faithful (Philippians 1:6).

Because we are so aware of our own sinfulness, it's hard to think that there can be one who is truly good. You and I doubt His goodness because we want to think of Him in human terms. We need to remember that He is pure; in Him there is no darkness (1 John 1:5). God *is* good. But there is yet another reason why we can rest and trust Him: He doesn't and could never act outside of His goodness. If God is love, then everything about Him is also good.

Implications for Us

We've surveyed the sovereignty, wisdom, love, and goodness of God. Now what do we do with this knowledge? We don't gain knowledge for knowledge's sake, because that puffs up (1 Corinthians 8:1). We gain knowledge of God to rightly worship and fear Him. We fear Him *because* we know Him—a knowing that is intimate and initiated by Him.

This knowing, which leads to trusting God, is taking all that knowledge and believing it to be true and putting it into action through prayer and rest. It is wise to trust the Lord. Remember that verse in Proverbs 1 about the fear of the Lord: "The fear of the LORD is the beginning of knowledge; fools despise wisdom and instruction" (v. 7). Wisdom is applying the knowledge, specifically, the Word of God.

And what we do will determine if we fear the Lord, so what is "fear of the Lord"?

.

Chapter 9

THE FEAR OF THE LORD

made mention a few chapters back that I'd return to the Proverbs 31 woman. I already know that many people are tired of her, and you might even be cringing at the thought of reading *anything* about her at all. I gave a talk recently in which I shared some insights I've picked up along the way about this poem found in Proverbs. The response to the talk was encouraging and slightly repetitive. Many women expressed something like this: "I have dreaded listening to talks on the Proverbs 31 woman. I can't measure up to that. After hearing your talk, I think I'm more encouraged to study her again." I don't share that to toot my own horn. I am sure I didn't deliver the words as well as I'd liked to. The truth is, the Proverbs 31 woman has been idolized, which is too bad. She's been used and abused. But no worries; I'm not going to talk merely about how excellent she is. I think that the Lord has something for us in those texts, and it isn't a to-do list.

So if you will lend me your ear—or in this case, your eyes—I believe that the Lord may have something for you too.

So why bother thinking about her? I'm thinking about one thing, and that is God's Word. In 2 Timothy 3:16–17 Paul tells us, "*All* Scripture is breathed out by God and profitable for *teaching*, for reproof, for correction, and for *training* in righteousness, that the man of God may be competent, equipped for every good work." God says His words are useful. That means that even if the "excellent wife" has been used and abused, His Word still stands true. The woman is an ideal we should look to; she is in a book dedicated to teaching wisdom. But don't make the mistake of making her out to be your small "god" and don't strive to be like her to the detriment of everything else in Scripture, thus piling on yourself condemnation when you fail. We don't want to do that. We can and should, however, look to her example, especially as it relates to the fear of the Lord.

The Proverbs 31 woman, also known as the "valiant woman" or the "excellent wife," is noble. She is respectful to her husband; she is trustworthy and kind; she is brave; she takes initiative; she works hard with her hands; she works inside and outside of the home; she is wise and respected. She is also generous and thoughtful. She is blessed by her children, and her children bless her.

But even with all those characteristics that make her definitely excellent, what we need to realize is that the most important aspect of the Proverbs 31 woman isn't what she does but whom she adores. Proverbs 31:30 says that she is a woman who fears the Lord. That is the climax of the entire poem. It isn't that she did all of life perfectly; it isn't that she did anything at all. The climax of the poem is that she feared the Lord. It reminds us that beauty is fleeting and vain, but a woman who fears the Lord is to be praised.

We see this same theme in 1 Peter 3:3–6. Peter, writing to Christians in the Roman provinces of Asia Minor, instructs the women:

> Do not let your adorning be external—the braiding of hair, the wearing of gold, or the putting on of clothing—but let your adorning be the hidden person of the heart with the imperishable beauty of a gentle and quiet spirit, which in God's sight is very precious. For this is how the holy women who hoped in God used to adorn themselves, by submitting to their own husbands, as Sarah obeyed Abraham, calling him lord. And you are her children, if you do good and do not fear anything that is frightening.

In the first century, jewelry signified wealth. So Peter is simply saying, "Don't be a show-off." Let your adorning be that of a gentle and quiet spirit.

So what is a gentle and quiet spirit? A gentle and quiet spirit is ultimately found in trusting and fearing the Lord. When describing a woman who possessed a gentle and quiet spirit, Peter uses the example of Sarah, who did not fear anything that was frightening. Who would have thought that so much of our womanhood would be wrapped up in this glorious calling to fear the Lord?

As we grow in our understanding of the goodness and sovereignty of God, which gives us the armor we need to stand in awe and reverence of the Lord rather than to walk in fear of our circumstances, our inward being begins to be transformed from anxiety to quietness, from angst to gentleness.[1] Fearing and knowing the Lord bring us the peace our heart craves.

But what does it mean to fear the Lord?

What Is the Fear of the Lord?

I remember that as I learned about God's sovereignty, I began to *fear* the Lord. I wondered if God was a tyrannical dictator and felt scared—maybe even terrified—as if God would rain down misery on my life, and I had no control over it. I realize I am not alone with this struggle and misunderstanding of what it means to fear the Lord. But, thankfully, this isn't what the fear of the Lord means at all.

John tells us in 1 John 4:18–19, "There is no fear in love, but perfect love casts out fear. For fear has to do with punishment, and whoever fears has not been perfected in love. We love because he first loved us." The fear that John is referring to here is the wrath of God or final judgment. My fear of the Lord was not rooted in thoughts of His love for me as His beloved daughter. Rather, I approached Him as if the wrath that He poured out on His Son on my behalf was still reserved for me. In other words, I had a difficult time reconciling the struggles and difficult circumstances I encountered with the love of God and instead feared that those struggles were indicators of His wrath. *Did I do something wrong?* I might think. This is not the way the Lord operates with those who love and fear Him. His wrath has been completely satisfied in Christ.

That's why, I believe, it's also important to understand that He is loving and kind, slow to anger and abounding in love. "The steadfast love of the Lᴏʀᴅ never ceases" (Lamentations 3:22).

The fear of the Lord, instead, can be manifested in many ways, but for our purposes it is to be understood as an awe and reverence of God, because we know that "the Lᴏʀᴅ is a great God, and a great King above all gods" (Psalm 95:3). The fear of the Lord starts in the heart. The outward expression of the fear of the Lord is obedience and fellowship and worship. Great is the Lord and greatly to be praised. The response to His awesomeness is to bow down in worship: "Oh come, let us worship and bow down; let us kneel before the Lᴏʀᴅ, our Maker!" (Psalm 95:6). Practically speaking, the fear of the Lord is manifested in obedience. During times when I am tempted to sin but don't, it isn't because of a natural inclination to do good; actually, Paul had it right when he said that when we desire to do good, sin is right there knocking on the door (see Romans 7:21). I obey the Lord because I have His Spirit, and I desire to honor Him. I fear Him.

To fear the Lord is not to be scared of Him. It's to adore Him. Worship Him. Honor Him. It's to put Him in the right place in our thinking. The fear of the Lord is in many ways to honor the first commandment: "You shall have no other gods before me" (Exodus 20:3; Deuteronomy 5:7); and to honor the Great Commandment: "You shall love the Lord your God with all your heart and with all your soul and with all your mind" (Matthew 22:37). Our response to our Creator is rejoicing, gratitude, and reverential fear. "Therefore let us be grateful for receiving a kingdom that cannot be shaken, and thus let us offer to God acceptable worship, with reverence and awe, for our God is a consuming fire" (Hebrews 12:28–29).

Chapter 10

WHEN YOUR FEARS COME TRUE

It was unexpected and swift, yet it seemed like an eternity. The phone rang: "Sis is in the hospital." Initially, I wasn't too concerned. I told my husband that it sounded serious but felt sure she would be released. Moments later, another call: "It doesn't look good." A few hours later: "She's gone."

I barely had time to process the reality of what had just happened. That was two years ago. It was her birthday—she was forty—and she had passed on to eternity. Needless to say, that night and the weeks ahead were difficult. I was tasked with caring and taking care of things that must be done when a loved one passes, which I'd never thought I'd need to do so soon. My older sis had a heart that broke and failed and took her life, and we were all left with broken hearts. My fear of premature loss and death, which I hoped would never come to pass, was coming true. We knew she was sick but had hoped for healing.

Over the past two years, I've mourned her death in various ways. There have been moments of incredible hope. I know one day death will be swallowed up. I know that death has already been defeated because of our Savior. The truth of these verses leaves me longing for heaven, anticipating the day when there will be no more tears or sorrow but, rather, rejoicing forevermore. That day is coming, and it will be glorious. And there have been days when my tears could fill a river. I weep for our loss. I have no words. Yes, I have hope, but I still feel an indescribable heaviness, so I don't try to explain. I simply cry.

Someone once said that if you live long enough, you *will* experience trials. Christianity doesn't promise ease; rather, God promises forgiveness and gives us rest, mercy, and grace. In His kindness, God also warns us that trials will come. And some of these trials may indeed be your worst fears come true. As I shared in chapter 4, I have had some of those fears come true. When that happens, then what? Is God still good? How do I reconcile His sovereignty with the trials in my life? How can fearing the Lord bring comfort and peace when your life fears come to pass?

You've trusted and waited, yet you remain single; you get married, and a few months later, you've lost your spouse. You've taken great care of your body your entire life, rarely get sick, catch what you think is a cold, go to the doctor, and discover you have bone cancer. You raise your kids in a stable, loving environment, you teach them the Scriptures, they grow up, and your son or daughter has become a prodigal. You get in financial trouble and lose your home. These aren't imaginary scenarios or simple illustrations. They are stories of the trials of my friends, people I know personally who have walked through difficulties despite all their attempts to live a certain way (e.g., healthy lifestyle, teaching kids the Word, waiting for marriage). Though all situations are very different, and each deserves unique attention, all require a level of trust in the Lord that can come only from the Spirit. Though I'm studying to become a counselor, I am not one, and some of these situations might be better helped by a trained professional. Nevertheless, I know that we all have the same Bible and the same gracious God to call upon during times of distress. My prayer is that the prior chapters provide the answer to the questions that arise in the midst of your fears coming true.

Knowing God and His Word allows us to face our fears with faith. We know that God is real. As the sun sets, fading behind the clouds and leaving a red-ray hue that lights the sky, there is no question that God is the transcendent Creator of the universe. Paul tells us that God's invisible attributes, namely, His eternal power and divine nature, have been clearly perceived ever since the creation of the world so we are without excuse (Romans 1:20). No one can truly deny the existence of God. Creation sings of God's majesty and mighty works. God's creation shouts His glory—yet another reminder that He is set apart, holy, and majestic.

And because God is different from us, we can trust Him fully. Along with His creation, God also reveals Himself through His Word. In Psalm 19, God's people celebrate the Law (the Torah) as His supreme revelation of Himself. The Lord's Word is perfect, refreshing, and reviving to the soul. It stands forever. The writer of Hebrews reminds us that the whole of Scripture is useful and perfect:

> For the word of God is living and active, sharper than any two-edged sword, piercing to the division of soul and of spirit, of joints and of marrow, and discerning the thoughts and intentions of the heart. And no creature is hidden from his sight, but all are naked and exposed to the eyes of him to whom we must give account. (Hebrews 4:12–13)

The Word is living, active, sharp, piercing, and discerning. It reveals the intentions of our heart. Christians experience this revelation of their hearts and an awareness of their depravity at the time of their salvation and throughout their Christian walk. As we understand the holiness and majesty of God and the commands of His perfect law as compared to our sinfulness, we can't help but discern our error and moral failures, as the psalmist did (Psalm 19:12–13). Like Isaiah, we humble ourselves and cry out: "Woe is me! For I am lost; for I am a man of unclean lips" (Isaiah 6:5).

And in the end, the psalmist offered up a sacrifice of acceptable words and meditations. You and I can often try to offer up our own sacrifices of good works in an effort to earn God's favor. But we no longer must offer up sacrifices, for the ultimate sacrifice has paid the price. Jesus is the friend of sinners. Jesus, the Son of God, died, fulfilling both the law and the promises of His coming. We can now receive His grace and sing Psalm 19 in celebration of His perfection and redemption.[1]

But we can't sing—we can't truly know the fullness of

all God has for us and *is* for us—if we don't first feast on the Word. We don't want to wait until our fears come true. We want to prepare now. You can read book after book, but it's only in God's Word that He is truly revealed, and it is there that He gives you the tools to face tragedies.

Because God is a generous and loving God, He also provides His Spirit and His Son to comfort us. Paul ensures us of this comfort:

> Blessed be the God and Father of our Lord Jesus Christ, the Father of mercies and God of all comfort, who comforts us in all our affliction, so that we may be able to comfort those who are in any affliction, with the comfort with which we ourselves are comforted by God. For as we share abundantly in Christ's sufferings, so through Christ we share abundantly in comfort too. If we are afflicted, it is for your comfort and salvation; and if we are comforted, it is for your comfort, which you experience when you patiently endure the same sufferings that we suffer. (2 Corinthians 1:3–6)

Like me, you will at some point in life experience loss (if you haven't already). If you live long enough, it is inevitable that someone you love dearly will slip away into eternity, and you will be left mourning, grieving, and enduring a trial that you may or may not have been fully prepared for. Though death brings a unique struggle and sting, it's not the only trial you will endure. But you will not be left to your own. Jesus will be your comfort, "for as we share abundantly in Christ's sufferings, so through Christ we share abundantly in comfort too."

Christ walked the earth perfectly on our behalf, but the Scriptures remind us that He did not walk it without hardship. I'm not referring to the greatest battle He endured (the cross). The writer of Hebrews says, "For we do not have a high priest who is unable to sympathize with our weaknesses, but one who in every respect has been tempted as we are, yet without sin" (Hebrews 4:15). Jesus was tempted for forty days by Satan (Mark 1:12–13). Isaiah, prophesying about the Lord, shares that Jesus, our perfect Savior, was despised and rejected by men; He was a man of sorrows and acquainted with much grief (Isaiah 53:3). Jesus knows suffering. He understands the sorrows of man.

We know His greatest suffering was indeed that of the cross. In His final moments on the cross, Mark records Him saying, "'Eloi, Eloi, lema sabachthani?' which means, 'My God, my God, why have you forsaken me?'" (Mark 15:34). His pain and suffering were for a purpose—the redemption of the world. He endured great pain, pain I can only scarcely imagine, pain and wrath on my behalf.

We share in Christ's sufferings for His name's sake. But we also receive comfort from Him through His Spirit and because of the gospel. Thankfully, we have a Savior who relates to our suffering. Jesus is aware of and acquainted with the grief of man. He is acquainted with my grief and your grief. And He wants to comfort you today by letting you know you are not alone. He is with you, interceding even now.

Comfort with the Comfort You've Received

There is something comforting in knowing that you are not alone in a struggle. The Scriptures call us to comfort with the comfort we've received. Jesus' pain and suffering were for a great purpose, and our pain and suffering serve a purpose as well. As Paul tells the Corinthians, one of the many purposes of suffering is that through it, we can now comfort with the comfort we've received from our Lord.

In this chapter I want to provide you with a few stories of women who have had their fears come true and how the Lord provided during those tough times. These stories ministered to me as I imagined myself in similar situations. The stories remind me that the Lord is near and that I can call out to Him in my time of need.

Donna: Loss of a Husband

My name is Donna Mitchell. My family and close friends call me DJ, and so did my late husband.

I'm fifty-four years old. I was married to Richard for twenty-three years, two months, and twenty-three days when he was killed in an automobile accident on January 30, 2004. He was forty-two. He was driving late at night, fell asleep at the wheel, and hit an eighteen-wheeler head-on. He was killed instantly. The truck ran down an embankment, but fortunately the driver was able to walk away.

When a tragedy like this happens, I have found that I *have* to start looking for God's hand in it and His mercy. My husband's boss (and great friend) and his wife drove to my house at 3 a.m. to deliver the news to me and my son, who was sixteen years old at the time. I called another church friend who lived close by, and she came over to be with me too. Our friends drove me and my son to Chattanooga to deliver the news to our two daughters, then twenty and twenty-two years old. I can remember praying the entire trip, and I believe God gave me a picture of myself sitting down, hugging my knees, head down, but in the palm of His mighty right hand. I was devastated, yet I knew I was in God's hand and that everything I was experiencing had carefully been sifted first through His hands.

There is an indescribable peace that comes from walking with the Lord through adversity. (God was pulling me most of the time.) Richard was a Christian, and I take great comfort in knowing that I will see him again someday. One of my greatest joys was seeing him worship in church, so now, when I'm sad, I am reminded of how he is worshiping in heaven.

It's been eleven years since Richard went home to be with the Lord. And though the years haven't been easy, God has remained faithful. Since that time, all three children have completed college, and I was able to go back and finish too. It's something my husband always wanted us all to do. God has shown me that He is my provider. He has shown me what His church body is and how He provides for us all through His believers. I thank God often for the friends that walked beside me through this trial. There are men in the church who have come alongside my son and mentored him. The singles and youth have served at my home doing projects. I've had financial and legal advice from men in the church who volunteered their time. I could go on and on! I see this as a practical way God is faithfully caring for me. I am grateful beyond words to Him for the way He has grown me and blessed me through this tragedy. He is who He says He is.

Anonymous: A Daughter and Pornography

When it comes to parenting my young children, I have many fears. All the "what ifs" can be so overwhelming when I consider my inexperience, lack of wisdom, my own sin, and the brokenness of the world we live in. But the Lord has been (and continues to be) kind to minister to me in my weakness. The fearful prospect of raising my children in our sex-obsessed culture is one area in which God has shown his mercy to me in my fears. When I read disturbing statistics about children and their exposure to pornography, it makes me feel like my guts are going to turn inside out.

My fears and God's kindness collided one afternoon, and His mercy prevailed. I left our living room and went to nurse my baby in the bedroom and returned a few minutes later to find that my first-grade daughter had opened a browser on my laptop and my iPad and searched for illicit images. Later she told me that she had gotten the idea from her best friend (another seven-year-old girl), who had admitted to my child that she had been watching "weird kissing" on her iPad before her parents awoke every morning. Out of sheer curiosity, my child decided she would try the Google search too, just to see what happened. When I realized the gravity of it all, it hit me that the very thing I had feared just happened in the span of a couple of minutes while I was in the next room. It was all too much to bear—I ran to the bathroom vomiting and crying. I begged the Lord for help, "Have mercy, God, they're only seven! Help, oh help! Protect these babies!"

When I came out of the bathroom, I picked up my iPad and examined the search history. My daughter tried to Google a phrase that her friend told her about, but multiple times she failed to spell those easy words correctly. Every search she attempted had failed because she didn't spell the words properly, and I saw how God's mercy had triumphed. To this day, I am humbled when I recall that afternoon, because I saw that the Lord is mighty to save and deliver the helpless ones. He protected my sweet girl when I was oblivious. Remembering His sovereign goodness leads me to humble myself before Him, repentant of my idolatry of control and the resulting fears of losing control.

Nikki: Fear of Man and a Marriage on the Rocks

Rewind to 2001, twelve years ago. I was twenty years old and full of the fear of man: insecure about my physical appearance, constantly comparing myself to other females, and never feeling loved. I was in my first serious relationship, which was full of jealousy and anger coming from my own heart. I'd be jealous if a pretty girl was sitting next to us at a restaurant and angry if my boyfriend so much as glanced toward her. Although a growing Christian, I was obsessed with what others thought of me and overcome with fear of not being enough.

While I clearly struggled to trust in the identity and worth I have in Christ, I found it simple to trust Christ in other, more burdensome areas. For example, I was ready to move overseas to the most dangerous areas of the world in order to share the gospel. If I died a martyr, I gained Christ! Isn't that bizarre? I felt at ease even in death but could not figure out how to trust Christ with the fear of man! In fact, I was trusting Christ in most areas, being challenged in the Word, under accountability with friends, and was "doing everything right," yet I still gave in time after time to the sinful fear of man.

My dating relationship ended after my boyfriend had had enough of my jealous rages and angry insecurities. A couple of years later, I met my future husband. I was able to hide my fear of man for a while, but it eventually came out during our engagement. The same fears I had dealt with previously burst out of my heart and colored themselves in bitter jealousy and out-of-control anger. I would explode and then apologize over and over again. It was a dark time in our relationship.

But, God . . . !

During our first year of marriage, my husband insisted on us seeing a biblical counselor together. I'd been thriving by demanding that my husband compliment me constantly. This was motivated by my fear that he would find another woman more attractive or interesting. I was terrified that he would cheat on me with someone who was taller with a curvier body. Although he never once gave me reason to believe these things would happen, the dark fear was deeply seeded in my heart. It didn't matter what my husband did or said; the fear was there and was not going away anytime soon.

So we began seeing a biblical counselor who quickly got to the heart of the problem: irrational fears. As a Christian, who am I to fear? God or man? It was so easy for me to fear man. It was natural for me. But to trust God in all circumstances, even when I felt ugly and unlovable? It seemed impossible! The things I saw as flaws were numerous: my nose was too big, my body too short, my hair too bland, my legs too thick, my voice too nasally—just to name a few. How was I to trust the Lord when all I could focus on was feeling like a big, unattractive mess?

In addition to counseling, my husband and I prayed together, read books and articles together, and grew in our trust of each other. It was a slow process, but I began to confess my feelings of fear right as they happened. I began to learn how to catch those feelings before they grew out of control. Once I caught them, I could confront them with the sharpest double-edged sword—the Word of God! I combated, "She's prettier than you, and your husband is going to notice," with, "Fear not, for I am with you; be not dismayed, for I am your God; I will strengthen you, I will help you, I will uphold you with my righteous right hand" (Isaiah 41:10). Suddenly, my heart was back to being focused on God instead of on myself! Later, I would see a skimpy girl flaunt her amazing body in front of my husband. Previously, I would have jumped to the conclusion that he must be lusting after her. But now I'd preach 2 Timothy 1:7 to myself: "For God gave us a spirit not of fear but of power and love and self-control" and trust my husband (who would quickly look at me and reassure me).

By the third year of marriage, my struggle with the fear of man was almost nonexistent. The Lord has used his powerful Scripture, a faithful husband, and biblical counseling to change me. Our marriage became marked by joy and peace instead of anger and jealousy.

By year eight, there is still a twinge of insecurity, but the overall banner in my life is trust in the Lord. What an amazing victory, and I cannot claim any glory for myself. I was the most messed-up sinner with very deep-rooted problems. Because of that, I love looking back over the last twelve years of my life and seeing the clear evidence of the Lord's incredible work. If left to myself, I would still be struggling with the same old insecurities and probably even to a deeper degree. But God had other plans, and for that I am forever grateful.

Katie: Singleness and the Fear of the Future

Fear of the unknown future torments so many people. As a single woman, I am no stranger to this. Specifically, I have experienced a lot of anxiety over the thought of being alone and independent for the rest of my life. As early as middle school, I remember being scared that one day the Lord would call me to singleness. I was terrified that I might, one day, have to rely on myself for everything. At that stage in life, I was used to being dependent on others. I had parents and older sisters whom I relied on for everything. I could not imagine one day being out on my own with no one to protect or provide for me. I remember nights praying desperately that the Lord would allow me to get married at a young age.

Once I graduated high school and went to college, I learned how to become more independent. However, I always saw my independence as a temporary thing. I hoped that by the time I graduated college (or shortly after),

I would be married. I had only to be on my own for a few years. And even then I wasn't truly independent, because my parents still financially supported me. Yes, I was learning independence in some aspects, but I was comforted in the fact that I was still relying on others.

College ended with no wedding, so I started seminary as a single. During this time, I had to become even more independent, but I still viewed this as a temporary status. Soon, I was sure to be married. However, as I neared the end of my seminary career, it looked like long-term singleness was going to be part of my future. I was almost crippled by fear as I realized that I might be on my own for the rest of my life. I was still terrified at the thought of being completely independent and having to rely on myself for everything. A lot of my friends were getting married, so fear and loneliness became all the more real. All of my life I had hoped to one day have a loving husband whom I could rely on for protection and provision. I was terrified that my future held only darkness, sadness, and loneliness. I would never feel complete. I would never feel secure. I would never truly feel important or loved.

Since graduating seminary in 2010, the Lord has taught me a great deal about singleness. He has shown me that it is actually an amazing and gracious gift from him. He has allowed me to truly understand and believe that He is always with me and has promised to never leave me. He has promised to care for me. He has promised to be my protection and provision. He has made me complete through His Son, Jesus Christ, and has graciously given me overwhelming comfort in Him. I now have this great peace in my singleness and even excitement to see how He uses it. I am no longer plagued by the idea of being by myself for the rest of my life. I am no longer terrified of being independent. Instead, I know that my independence is really my complete dependence on God for everything I need.

Of course, not all my fears have subsided. I still experience some uneasiness from not really knowing what the future holds. I may no longer be crippled by the fear of never getting married, but there are still fears that creep in with the thought of being single long-term. Does it mean I will have to stay at my current job for the rest of my life? Does it mean the Lord will call me to go do something completely out of my comfort zone? Will I really be as useful to the kingdom being single as those who are married? Or what if God does eventually call me to marriage? Will I be so used to my independence that I am not able to be a submissive wife? In spite of these lingering fears, at the end of the day, I choose to trust the Lord's sovereignty. I choose to trust him when He says He will bring to completion what He has started in me (Philippians 1:6). I choose to trust His promise that everything that happens in my life truly is for my good (Romans 8:28). I choose to trust His promise of providing for my every need (Luke 12:22–31). And, above all, I choose to glorify Him in all circumstances for the purpose of shedding His light and truth to this fallen and broken world.

Lindsey: The Loss of a Friend and the Fear of Rejection

I feared friendship because I'd experienced one crumble after I unintentionally said something hurtful to a dear friend. Despite my apologies and repentance, my words could not repair the damage that had been done. Things just weren't the same. She went her way, and I went mine, and the parting broke my heart. Because of this one misunderstanding, my foolishness, and her rejection, I became frightened in all my friendships.

The fear of disappointing, hurting, or losing another friend caused me to build walls of self-protection around my heart. I avoided authenticity and vulnerability with long-time friends because I was afraid of being too open, afraid of messing up, and afraid of being misunderstood. Ultimately, I was afraid of getting hurt again, so I rejected others before they could reject me.

Protecting myself proved to be a pretty lonely endeavor. I missed having the love and support of friends and being involved in their lives. I missed knowing how to pray for them and the comfort of knowing they were praying for me too. It turns out that I couldn't live behind the walls I'd built. Through pain, the Lord has taught me that friendship is a risk worth taking, not because people are trustworthy, but because He is trustworthy. Even if I get hurt, He redeems all things. Because He has called me to fellowship with other believers, I must fight all fear that keeps me from investing in relationships.

When I can't fix a relationship, when I'm hurt or rejected, I still have hope. God can be trusted to fight for relational restoration even when people aren't willing. I know God can be trusted to redeem the messiest relationships because He sent His Son to redeem a mess like me. Because Christ suffered the worst pain, my relational suffering is an invitation to have fellowship with Christ. My pain is an opportunity to glorify God as I experience conflict and suffering. Because of the gospel, my worst-case scenario is no longer rejection or losing friends. I can trust God's sovereignty in my relationships, so I have no need to fear.

———— ✦ ————

These are stories of waiting, loss, and fear. You may not experience these particular struggles and trials, but doesn't it build your faith to see God's faithfulness in the lives of real people? This is real life, folks. You are not alone, because of our God; and you are not alone, because so many have gone before you in their own pain. These women are eager to share their stories with you in order to proclaim Jesus and comfort you with the comfort they've received.

I mentioned that the Word of God will help guide and shield us when our fears come true. But we know that much of what we fear may never come to pass. As I mentioned previously, your fears may be a result of a scenario that you've created in your imagination. At the moment, in the midst of crippling fear, it can seem so real. So how might we fight those fears that come true only in our mind? Using the Word as her guide and shield, Megan shares how she lost her husband in her mind one night and how the Lord comforted her.

Megan: The Night Rob Died

I was doing the dishes. And with every clink of fork on knife, with every squeak of my sponge on glass, I hopefully imagined the shutting of a car door in the dark driveway, the turning of the key in the front door, the shuffling of muddy size-fourteens on the doormat. But the gleaming plates piled up, warm and damp, and I remained alone.

Where was he? Was he dead?

I had always been afraid of losing my husband, and this night was no different. Inside my wedding ring were the words "heir with Rob," a reference to 1 Peter 3:7: "Husbands, live with your wives in an understanding way . . . since they are heirs with you of the grace of life." From the day my minister-dad had pronounced us husband and wife, I believed we had received the grace of life. But I also constantly remembered "'til death do us part," and for the past nine years I had known that truth too. In the midst of life together, we were in death.

I could never imagine life without him, my husband, lover, friend, and brother. And with the addition of each child to our family, my fear of his death had grown. With three little boys burrowed under covers, my need for my husband amounted to desperation.

When Rob didn't come home when he had promised, when he didn't answer his phone, when the clock ticked off the minutes and the darkness descended, I entered into deeper and deeper fear. I was afraid of the car wreck that had recently widowed another pastor's wife, the sudden cardiac arrest that took a friend's husband at age thirty-two, the flash floods and bullets and freight trains that failed to signal their approach but which left names in the newspaper, all the same.

I finished the dishes and let the water drain out of the sink, hung up the towel, and reached with water-shriveled fingers for my Bible.

What if he's dead, Lord? What if he never comes through that door? Will You still be good to me?

And the Spirit, the one Jesus called "the Comforter," turned my heart toward Romans 8:38–39: "I am sure that neither death nor life, nor angels nor rulers, nor things present nor things to come, nor powers, nor height nor depth, nor anything else in all creation, will be able to separate us from the love of God in Christ Jesus our Lord." Neither life nor death.

If my husband were dead, it would change everything. This particular grace of life—with nightly dinner and long hugs and shared prayer—would end. And yet it would change less than I might think. I would still be united to Christ. I would still be loved by the Father.

But why, Lord? Why would you let him die?

And again the Spirit prompted me. I flipped pages until I found 1 Peter 1:6–7: "In this you rejoice, though now for a little while, if necessary, you have been grieved by various trials, so that the tested genuineness of your faith—more precious than gold that perishes though it is tested by fire—may be found to result in praise and glory and honor at the revelation of Jesus Christ." If necessary.

I remembered how my brother, facing a trial of his own, had choked through tears, "God wouldn't have done this if there were an easier way." The death of my husband would not be a senseless act of a negligent God. The death of my husband would happen only if necessary. Necessary for His glory. Necessary for my good.

Once, sheltering from a tornado, my four-year-old son had prayed, "Dear God, I'm not asking you to keep us safe.

I'm asking you to do what is right." Standing in my silent kitchen, I borrowed his prayer.

I'm not asking for Rob to be alive. I'm asking for what is right. And if this trial is necessary, I will take it from your hand and trust you to show me some kindness in it.

Years later, I often think about that night. I call it "The Night Rob Died," though he is still very much alive. Eventually, he walked in with an explanation of traffic or pastoral crisis or who-remembers-what.

Rob didn't die that night, but my fear of his death did.

And one day recently, I thought I had lost not my husband but my son. He was there, and then he wasn't. And though I walked the perimeter of that soccer field three times looking for a freckled nose and a yellow T-shirt, I couldn't find him. My heart wavered, but the Spirit was there too, and I talked to myself as I walked, repeating with each step until I saw my little boy: *If necessary. If necessary. If necessary.*

---- ◆ ----

When your fears come true, you must remember Jesus. He has not left you to weather the storm alone. That doesn't mean there won't be a storm, but He will be with you through it. In the midst of the trials of this life, I'm often reminded of Jesus in the boat with His disciples. It's a familiar story, found in Mark 4:35–41. The disciples climb in a boat and take off on the Sea of Galilee. The Sea of Galilee was known for sudden and violent storms.[2] So, when the storm approached, it brought crashing waves strong enough to wash over into the boat. The disciples were terrified. Jesus, on the other hand, was asleep. He wasn't worried about the raging seas. His disciples, however, woke Him in a frenzy saying, "Teacher, do you not care that we are perishing?" Jesus decided to remind them who He was and why they could trust Him. With a word He stopped the storm, "Peace! Be still!" and they were filled with great fear but no longer the misappropriated fear of the storm. They were now filled with an awestruck wonder of Jesus—the God-man—and the disciples proclaimed, "Who then is this, that even wind and sea obey him?" They now feared rightly.

During our storms, you and I have the same God with us that the disciples had with them; we can trust that He is in the boat. He may or may not calm the storm immediately— we may have to endure great suffering—but He will not leave us. One of my favorite hymns, "Jesus, Savior, Pilot Me," does a magnificent job of capturing the truth of God's sovereignty and goodness during the storms of life. In the song, they acknowledge that the waves are raging, and they cry out to God with this lyric: "Chart and compass come from Thee; / Savior, pilot me. . . . / May I hear you say to me, / I will pilot thee."[3]

Our good, loving, sovereign God will pilot us. His love never ceases, and He is great in faithfulness. "'The LORD is my portion,' says my soul, 'therefore I will hope in him'" (Lamentations 3:24). May this be the cry of our heart when our fears come true.

Chapter 11

GROWING IN THE FEAR OF THE LORD

B y now we've realized our tendency to fear and seen the One we can trust, yet we are left to wonder, how can we grow? When thinking about growth, I typically go back to one verse: Philippians 1:6.

As Paul so often did, he begins his letter to the church in Philippi with a prayer of thanksgiving. Paul was such an encourager. Sure, he knocked a few heads, but nothing he said, inspired by the Spirit, was out of selfishness. He loved greatly. So what did he say to this church? He tells them (and us) that "I am sure of this, that he who began a good work in you will bring it to completion at the day of Jesus Christ." The Christian is not left to grow on her own. God began the work in you, and He will finish it. He will teach you to fear Him. The work of growing in the Lord will culminate in a complete, joy-filled, perfect fear of the Lord on the day you see Jesus. You can and should actively seek this growth, by the grace of God, knowing that nothing you do will earn your righteous standing before the Lord.

Here are a few ways you can actively seek to grow in the fear of the Lord.

Confession

My friend and I sat across from each other attempting a conversation that we both knew would happen only short of a miracle. Our kids jumped and wiggled beside us as we encouraged them to eat their Chick-fil-A, the food of choice for moms with young kids. As they settled down into their seats and short moments of silence emerged, I looked at my girlfriend and busted out, "I've got to get out of my head." Without even a blink, she instantly understood me.

Each day as I labor to serve my children, I am alone in my home and often left to my thoughts. From my head come the sins that are often manifested in being quick-tempered, snappy, impatient, grumbling, or even tearful. It's a dangerous place up there—at times. Outwardly I can appear to have it together, while inwardly, in my secret thoughts, I can be tempted to fear and anxiety. I can covet, and I can long to be other places, leaving me discontented.

I can think at times that my thoughts are my own. No one will know my thoughts unless I tell them. No one but me can see that I am judging the motive of another. No one knows that I'd prefer at this moment to be in Paris, sipping on a café au lait, rather than sweeping this floor for the hundredth time. Oh, my discontentment is just in my head, I can think.

But the Lord knows. He knows the thoughts of man.

Even His Word discerns the thoughts and intentions of the heart (Hebrews 4:12). And when I look back at a week of unhelpful, unfruitful thoughts, I rejoice in knowing that God's thoughts aren't my thoughts (Isaiah 55:8–9).

Yet God has given me His Spirit, and by His grace He will sanctify my thoughts. I can be tempted in my thoughts, but I do not have to sin. I can take my thoughts captive and put on righteousness in the secret places of my soul. And when He saved me, He left nothing uncovered and unclothed with Christ's righteousness. He saves to the uttermost—to the depths of our soul and the darkest places (Hebrews 7:25).

So as I confessed my thoughts to my friend, I rejoiced in knowing that what was now in the light had already been known by God and had already been forgiven by God. This is the same for our fears. In his book *Running Scared*, Ed Welch says, "Rather than minimize our fears, find more of them. Expose them to the light of day because the more you find, the more blessed you will be when you hear words of peace and comfort."[1]

The point is that because God is holy and all-knowing, I should fear Him. But because I know He is also loving and good, I can be open and honest about my sin. Confession is an active way of displaying your trust and fear of the Lord. You fear Him, so you confess your sins. And as you saw in my little example, these are things God already knows; nothing surprises Him. Because you fear Him and are most concerned with Him, you don't have to fear your friend's opinion of you. Doesn't that sound like freedom? What grace! We can actively pursue the fear of the Lord through confessing our sins to one another and receiving the grace available to us.

Remember His Promises

Because we know God and because we fear God, we can trust God. There is only one God, and He is our Father. He most clearly reveals Himself in His Word, so it is there that we must turn to learn more about Him and grow in fearing Him. We see His words written on everything from bumper stickers to Hallmark cards, but we can't miss that they are the words of life and that they are trustworthy.

In *Taking God at His Word*, Kevin DeYoung lays out why we can trust and believe God's Word. He says that God's Word says what is true. God's Word demands what is right. But it is his third point that is most relevant to me. I think we can believe His Word and even believe that we need to obey it. But do we believe it provides what is *good*? He writes:

> According to Psalm 119, the word of God is the way of happiness (vv. 1–2), the way to avoid shame (v. 6), the way of safety (v. 9), and the way of good counsel (v. 24). The word gives us strength (v. 28) and hope (v. 43). It provides wisdom (vv. 98–100, 130) and shows us the way we should go (v. 105). . . . As the people of God, we believe the word of God can be trusted in every way to speak what is true, command what is right, and provide us with what is good.[2]

God's Word is good and provides what is good for us. God's Word is sufficient for us to fight temptation and to know Him. He has given us all we need for life and godliness (2 Peter 1:3). We gain wisdom from the Word, and, as DeYoung writes, "The word of the world is not like the word of God. One is new and now. The other is ancient and ever-lasting. . . . If we want—and if we *need*—a wisdom that is beyond us, that is outside of us, that will never fail us, we must look into the things that 'God has revealed to us through the Spirit' [1 Corinthians 2:10]."[3] Because of these things we can trust Him and take Him at His word.

So we can rest and remember these and many more promises:

Oh, how abundant is your goodness, which you have stored up for those who fear you and worked for those who take refuge in you, in the sight of the children of mankind! (Psalm 31:19)

The LORD takes pleasure in those who fear him, in those who hope in his steadfast love. (Psalm 147:11)

He fulfills the desire of those who fear him; he also hears their cry and saves them. (Psalm 145:19)

Behold, the eye of the LORD is on those who fear him, on those who hope in his steadfast love. (Psalm 33:18)

Why all this talk about the Word of God? Because at the root of our fear, at the root of all our sin, is unbelief. In order to combat our unbelief, you and I must believe, and so we turn to God to ask Him to help our unbelief.

Our ability to grow in the fear of the Lord is sitting right there on our nightstand. We turn to Scripture and learn about the Lord. I found myself at a crossroads many years ago. Either I would believe that what God said in His Word about His children and, most importantly, Himself, is true, or I would continue to trust my own feelings, fears, and thoughts. God began to work in me a renewed vision of Him that was rooted in what He has revealed about Himself in Scripture. What God truly renewed in my mind and heart was a fear of Him.

Fear Not

One way to grow in the fear of the Lord is not to fear other things at all. Obviously, we will continue to fear, but as we grow in trusting God and fearing Him, we will rightly place our fears on Him. We will begin to fear less, not be fearless. Remember, we are being changed from one degree of glory to another. We are being transformed into the image of our Lord—and it's a process, a process of growth overtime (2 Corinthians 3:18).

Depending on your Bible translation, there could be well over three hundred verses that contain the phrase "fear not." One of the most popular occurrences is found in Isaiah 41:10: "Fear not, for I am with you; be not dismayed, for I am your God; I will strengthen you, I will help you, I will uphold you with my righteous right hand."

All of Isaiah 41 points to God's sovereign hand. And then in the middle of it, He reminds us that He is not only sovereign but also loving, good, and for us, and because of this we do not need to fear. God is with us.

So when our fear of man seems louder than our trust in Him, or our fear for the future overwhelms our thoughts, or our fear and comparison strip us of our joy, the Lord pro-claims to us, "Fear not, I am with you." He reminds us that He is our God. He is a personal and intimate God. He knew us before the foundation of the earth, and He knit us together in the womb of our mother.

When your fears tell you that you are alone, God whis-pers, "I am your God." He will uphold you. He has adopted us as His children. He sent His Son to die for us. He loves us with an everlasting love. He has covenanted with us.

Your fears tell you that you have to be strong. God tells you, "I will strengthen you."

Your fears will tell you that you will fall and fail. Your fears will tell you that you have to muster up the strength to be all that you think the Lord desires you to be, and that you must do it on your own. Your fears will tell you that you don't measure up and never will. God tells you, "I will uphold you with my righteous right hand."

Your fears will tell you to fear. God tells you, "Be not dismayed."

There's an old hymn that sums up well this section and, really, this entire chapter. It is one of my favorite hymns, "How Firm a Foundation." This foundation is the Word of God, the foundation of knowing our Father so that we can rest and trust and fear rightly.

How firm a foundation, ye saints of the Lord,
Is laid for your faith in His excellent Word!
What more can He say than to you He hath said,
You, who unto Jesus for refuge have fled?
In every condition, in sickness, in health;

In poverty's vale, or abounding in wealth;
At home and abroad, on the land, on the sea,
As thy days may demand, shall thy strength ever be.
Fear not, I am with thee, O be not dismayed,
For I am thy God and will still give thee aid;
I'll strengthen and help thee, and cause thee to stand
Upheld by My righteous, omnipotent hand.
When through the deep waters I call thee to go,
The rivers of woe shall not thee overflow;
For I will be with thee, thy troubles to bless,
And sanctify to thee thy deepest distress.
When through fiery trials thy pathways shall lie,
My grace, all sufficient, shall be thy supply;
The flame shall not hurt thee; I only design
Thy dross to consume, and thy gold to refine.
Even down to old age all My people shall prove
My sovereign, eternal, unchangeable love;
And when hoary hairs shall their temples adorn,
Like lambs they shall still in My bosom be borne.
The soul that on Jesus has leaned for repose,
I will not, I will not desert to its foes;
That soul, though all hell should endeavor to shake,
I'll never, no never, no never forsake.[4]

God's patience with you and me—His children—is astounding. It reminds me once again of His great love for us. He knows that sanctification is a process, and it is only by His grace that we ever grow and change. Even with all I know about the Lord and all I have learned about the nature of fear, I still continue to fear. But as I've walked longer in the faith, I have learned how to take captive the fear-inducing, gripping thoughts that once led me down a spiral of despair. I've learned how to repent more quickly and cling harder to Jesus. I've learned that if all my fears were to come to pass, I would still have my Savior. Ultimately, I've learned what it means to rest in the implications of the gospel, and that, I believe, is growth in the fear of the Lord.

And that is what I am praying for you. This walk, this Christian journey, is truly a walk of faith. It may be that the Lord gives you the faith to trust Him during your trial, with your fear, or in your dark valley immediately, or it may be that day and night, you continually ask for new faith. Either way the Lord loves you the same today, yesterday, tomorrow, and forevermore. His character doesn't change, and His great love for you doesn't change. He will give you Himself as you ask Him. Ask the Lord to reveal Himself to you.

Pastor and author Jerry Bridges is known for saying that he preaches the gospel to himself every day, and he encourages other Christians to do the same. I've always appreciated his advice and focus on the sufficiency of the gospel. I also realize that I'm forgetful and *need* to preach it to myself each day. I imagine that you may experience the same sort of forgetfulness that I do. Many mornings when we wake up, it seems that the cards are stacked against us. Add in the trials of life and fears, and it can be quite overwhelming. Enter forgetfulness. It is for this reason that I want to remind you even now why we can run to God with our fears.

God is sovereign. He is reigning over the universe. He is holy and majestic—a mighty God we can trust. God is not only sovereign and holy; He is personally and intimately acquainted with you and all of your needs. He knows what you need before you utter a word. He knows what you need when you don't even know what you need. But He isn't only acquainted with you, He loves you. His love is pure and eternal. His love is indescribable. He loves you with an everlasting, life-giving love. He sent His Son to die for you—that's how much He loves you. He is a good God and has no evil intentions. He can't do evil, so you can trust that He will do good for you. So I join Paul in asking and reminding you:

> What then shall we say to these things? If God is for us, who can be against us? He who did not spare his own Son but gave him up for us all, how will he not also with him graciously give us all things? Who shall bring any charge against God's elect? It is God who justifies. Who is to condemn? Christ Jesus is the one who died—more than that, who was raised—who is at the right hand of God, who indeed is interceding for us. Who shall separate us from the love of Christ? Shall tribulation, or distress, or persecution, or famine, or nakedness, or danger, or sword? (Romans 8:31–35)

Nothing can separate us from Him and His love—not our fears, not our trials. We can run to God confidently because of Jesus. Take your fears to Him, the one who can carry your burden. He wants you to truly know Him. He is the only place you and I can come and find true rest. He is worthy of your faith and trust.

Appendix 1

EATING DISORDERS

One Girl's Story of Anorexia and the Mercy of God
by Eva Crawford

I was saved at a young age, grew up in a Christian family, and was involved in a great church. I believed in God, prayed, sang songs, and sought to obey and please Him. However, at a young age (despite being taught this truth), I never grasped how deceitful and depraved my own heart was (and is!). I was a little legalist who knew the right answers and was proud of it. I remember distinctly standing in Walmart as a child, knowing that I wasn't supposed to look at the magazine racks by the register, but thought I was mature enough to handle whatever was on them. I read a line saying, "Cheated on her . . . murdered," and thought, *I'm so glad I'm not that bad.* Grace wasn't amazing to me. Subconsciously, I thought sin had categories, and I just wasn't that bad. I really do believe I was a Christian as a child, but I was incredibly proud and self-righteous.

Anorexia was stupid. "How could a girl starve herself?" I would ask.

As I grew outwardly (puberty, etc.), my craving for others' approval and self-righteousness also grew. I believed I could control my life, schedule, and appearance, and I looked down my nose at others who didn't have as much self-control. I was always active and thin growing up, but somewhere around fourteen or fifteen my approval-craving tendencies began to show me how much positive attention I received from being thin, athletic, disciplined, self-controlled, and toned. As my body changed in those teen years (hips happened), I began to work out regularly to stay in shape, but my activity was fueled by a desire to be praised and well thought of. The possibility of being overly obsessed never crossed my mind.

As I lost weight, a small nodule on my neck became exposed. My parents took me to doctors to have it checked, and the doctors thought it was possibly a thyroid issue. My thyroid was just fine, but my heart was a mess. The doctors were aware that I was thin and asked about it, but I just shrugged it off. The weight kept coming off, and my obsession with what I termed "healthy," "disciplined," and "self-controlled" grew all the more. I was self-righteously blind to my enslavement. The drive to work out and my anxious, angry response when I wasn't able to revealed what my heart treasured: myself.

The so-called control and discipline I thought I had achieved over everyone else were killing me. My self-controlled disciplines fueled self-righteousness toward anyone who couldn't be as disciplined as I was. I was five feet ten and lost weight gradually over a ten-month period until, at my lowest, I weighed ninety pounds. Even in the depth of my sin, I was self-righteous. I remember thinking, *Who would ever make themselves throw up to lose weight?* So I never went the route of vomiting, but instead I engaged in rigorous, secret workout routines to burn off the carefully calculated calories I had consumed during the day. Of course, if I missed a day or forgot a few reps, I would have to do double to make up for it later. My mind and heart were consumed with what I ate and how to burn it off. My "self-control and discipline" idolatry had driven me into enslavement beyond what I could ever control. Worst of all, I was blind to it and still thought I was better than others.

My parents, on the other hand, were not blind. To this day, I can't imagine how a parent would feel watching his or her child starve herself. But they weren't just watching or passive. They cared for me physically, took me to doctors, tried to curb my exercise, tried to get calories in me, and more. However, the thing I'm most thankful for is how they patiently cared for my soul during this time. They saw the outward destruction I was doing to my body, but they went deeper because they knew my problem was ultimately a heart issue. Our culture says it's due to low self-esteem or that people "get anorexia" (as if it's a bug going around), but my parents went straight to my heart and motives. They continually pointed me to Scripture, took me to meet with a pastor, prayed for me, and visited with other Christian girls who struggled. The pain, heartache, and burden put on my family during this season is hard for me to reflect on and imagine. Their patience astounds me even today.

During that season, almost any time with the family with or without food was incredibly challenging because of my idolatry and usually ended with me crying or getting angry.

Even in the midst of denying my idolatry, the Lord faithfully pursued and convicted my soul. I had grown up subtly thinking that the Lord loved me *because* I was a good girl. But my life had become characterized by anger, lying, misery, exhaustion, striving, and slavery to my idol of control. Through a variety of people, the Lord slowly opened my eyes to the depth of blindness and deceit in my own heart. Prior to this time, I had prided myself on being truthful, but now my life had become a lie of wasted food and secret exercise. I had thought of myself as patient and kind, but now I went into angry tirades if I was forced to eat something I didn't want to. I knew these things in my life were wrong, yet I didn't care because I was so enslaved by my desire for control. The Lord in His mercy gently revealed that the god I was really serving in my actions and life was very different from what I proclaimed with my mouth.

I remember being aware that I had a choice to either continue down this path or trust the Lord. For the first time, I was struck by the grace of God—why would He give me a choice? He could let me die; yet in the very depth and deceitfulness of my sin, He pursued me. For the first time I really began to see that Eva was an adulterous hater of Him. Yet He was willing to die for me. Even though I had heard it all my life, I was really aware, perhaps for the first time, of the depth of wickedness in my own heart and how even my righteousness was filthy before Him. Grace became sweet. The gospel became real to me like never before. Change wasn't easy, but the Lord poured out grace once again. I discovered that He's the only master who brings lasting joy instead of enslavement.

I couldn't trust myself anymore. I was terrified by the feeling of lacking control that often accompanies weight gain. I feared being fat but was aware that somehow, even though I wasn't in control, there was joy and freedom that I hadn't known before in trusting the Lord. Gradually, within three to four months, I was back to a healthy weight. My body went back to normal. My blood levels balanced, and my menstrual cycle returned. Doctors were surprised by how quickly that happened. Truly it was the mercy of God.

I wish I could say that I am 100 percent free from ever being concerned about my appearance, my craving for approval, and my self-righteousness. Far from that, there are still days that I wake up and have to question my motives for eating and working out and my works/control mentality. It's something I will likely have to fight to some degree for the rest of my life. As I reflect on this season of my life almost six years later, it's hard to discern exactly what I was learning then and where I am now, but one strong cord runs through all the memories: the mercy of God toward a sinner like me.

An Open Letter to My Friends Struggling with Eating Disorders by Emily Wierenga

I want to take you back twenty years, to when I am thirteen years old.

I am a pastor's kid standing in a hospital room with clumps of hair in my hand.

My nails are splintered, and you can see the outline of my braces through my cheeks.

I weigh sixty pounds.

The room smells like Lysol. Nurses say I'm dying.

I was brushing my hair when it started to fall, and I tried to catch all the falling pieces and put them back on my head.

Today I ate for the first time in four years—truly ate, everything on my plate, everything they put before me—because even though I still don't think I have anorexia, I know this isn't normal.

To be purple from hypothermia and unable to run or lift objects and to have your friends cry when they see you—this is not normal.

It will be another twenty years before I can admit to having a mental illness, but today is a start. Because I saw *her* on the way to the hospital. A woman, jogging, and she was muscular and the most beautiful woman I'd ever seen. She seemed fully alive.

And I realized, then, in that moment, that I was hungry for more than food.

I had been starving long before I ever refused my first meal.

I had no idea about anorexia nervosa. We were preacher's kids, raised singing hymns and memorizing Scripture, and homeschooled at our parents' long, wooden table. The only TV we watched was a black-and-white one we found at the dump. We pulled it up from the basement once a week for Sunday-night Disney. I wasn't allowed to take dance classes or look at fashion magazines because Mum, who was a nutritionist, thought they might trigger an eating disorder.

But darkness, like light, leaks in through the cracks.

And if we're forced to deny our sin from the day we're born, we'll never realize we need a Savior. We'll only ever punish ourselves for not being what we feel we're supposed to be: perfect.

I had only ever been a good girl, quiet unless spoken to. I took care of my younger siblings. I spent hours on my poems and my pictures, hoping to earn the attention of a father who spent most of his time at the church or in his office.

I was never asked what my favorite color was. I didn't know my favorite color until I was married, a seemingly small thing until you realize it's not just that—you also don't know how you like your eggs done, or your steak, or what your favorite shampoo is, because all you know was that it has to be inexpensive.

It's the small things that eventually add up to become the big picture of why you don't love yourself.

And when I was thirteen and standing there in that green hospital gown, Mum telling me in her soft British accent that nurses said I was a miracle because I was still alive (I should have died), it felt like God reaching down and cupping my cheeks and saying, "I will never leave you nor forsake you."

It was my heavenly Father reassuring me there was more to life than rules and liturgies. There was joy—and it tasted good.

Friend, have you tasted that joy?

I finally knew, in spite of the pain of my childhood and the clumps of hair in my hand, that God loves me because He made me. And even more, because He died for me. And suddenly my body was no longer just skin covering muscle covering bone. It was a vessel, and God wanted to pour His love into me so I could pour it into others. We are not just physical beings. We are spiritual, and part of me always knew this, and this is why food was never enough.

But it took relapsing one more time into anorexia as a young married woman to not only acknowledge God's love for me but also let it fill me, because joy is not found in a perfect life. Joy is the peace that transcends all understanding as we look into the eyes of our Maker and see that we can trust Him in spite of the pain around us. God is trustworthy.

Leftovers

I used to think the famous miracle in John 6 was all about bread, fish, and five thousand empty stomachs that needed dinner. Yet I always found myself perplexed about why Jesus would allow such waste—why He'd create twelve baskets of leftovers.

But that's to miss the point. The story is not about bread or fish.

As Jesus later explained to the crowd, "I am the bread of life; whoever comes to me shall not hunger, and whoever believes in me shall never thirst" (John 6:35).

Jesus is the bread. He is the eternal sustenance for the hungry soul. In Him our souls no longer go hungry or thirsty. The leftovers in the story are a picture for us, reminding us every time we read it that He is more than enough for you and more than enough for every need in my life.

To feed on living bread is to find Christ sufficient for every hunger pang I feel in my soul, to let His grace and goodness fill all the empty, aching places inside of me, to nourish and grow me strong in faith and love.

Friend, do you know this living bread?

Five Truths

I know, it's not easy: when the world tells you that you are what you eat or what you weigh or that you're only as good as your calorie count or the number of followers on social media.

The world weighs with numbers; the Lord weighs with grace, and you owe Him nothing, friend. Everything and nothing. He has paid it all. He wants you to rest and trust him. He's got you covered. Here are five truths I want you to tuck into your heart today and carry with you.

1. You have a voice. I know your eating disorder seems to be in control right now, and you can't stop thinking about it, yet the truth is that in one breath, you can surrender your eating disorder. It does not control you. You have a voice, and you can use it to stand up against anorexia in the name of Jesus. But until the issues that are driving your eating disorder are addressed—the longing to be seen and heard and held, the pain of being hurt by people who say they love you—E.D. will remain a deceptively safe place. A wall to hide behind.

Please know that it's not what it seems. God sees you; He hears you; He is holding you. You are free through the power of Christ to declare victory over your eating disorder right now.

2. You can be free of anorexia forever. There is a lie circling the planet that tells us, "Once mentally ill, always mentally ill," and I believed it for years. I relapsed because of it, and then one day I realized, no, the Bible declares us to be a new creation in Christ. It says the old has passed away, the new has come. It talks about being transformed by the renewing of your mind (Romans 12:2).

We no longer need to subscribe to the rules of the world. Yes, we do have to be aware of our triggers and careful of temptations, as does everyone; we cannot be foolish, but we can also trust Isaiah 54:17, which says that no weapon formed against us shall prosper. We can be free of our eating disorders—completely free—forever, because of the power of Jesus Christ at work within us.

3. You are more than your eating disorder. You, friend, are not your eating disorder. I know you cling to it for protection, but your identity is being consumed rather than identified. Your E.D. has become your idol, and it's only when you see it for what it is—a lie from the enemy, who wants God's sons and daughters to die—that you will be free to pursue the dreams God has for you. Eating disorders are a spiritual battle, and I believe Satan attacks young men and women who have been called by Jesus to move mountains. I believe that you, friend, have been called to do something mighty in your life, and Satan is using this E.D. as a distraction so that you cannot step into the plans God has for you. You are more than your E.D. You are more than a conqueror in Jesus (Romans 8:37). Your identity is now defined and determined forever by your union with Christ.

4. You are not crazy. I know you feel like you are. All those voices warring in your head, and you're so tired of hearing them, and you wish life could be over. Please don't give up. You're not going crazy. You're just hungry—hungry for food, yes, but also hungry to know why you're alive and what your purpose is. You long for spiritual worth and meaning. Those voices can be muted by one soft whisper, the whisper of a God who will fight for you if you let Him. Call out to Jesus, and He will silence Satan's control over your thoughts. Read Scripture and remind yourself of the truth of who God says you are, as declared by Zephaniah 3:17: delighted in, sung over, and quieted with His love.

5. The rest of your life is not determined by this moment. Friend, I know it feels like this is it, that your life will be marred by this period of time spent battling anorexia, but it doesn't have to be that way. When I was thirteen, doctors said I probably wouldn't be able to have children due to the damage I'd done to my body. When I turned twenty-seven, I was prayed over by a pastor who prayed that I would be able to conceive a son within the year, and I did. I now have two little boys and am pregnant with my third.

When you serve the almighty Creator, nothing is impossible—He can give you the desires of your heart. But you need to surrender; you need to invite Him in to begin the healing so that every single one of those days can be restored.

The Ache

This world is not our home, friends. It's the ache that pulses within you, the cry of the Spirit of the Son for His Abba Father.

We're homeless beggars, leading each other to the living bread, and I'm walking there with you. Can you feel me holding your hand?

We're almost there. Step by shaky step.

Your friend and sister, a former anorexic who now defines herself as a victor in Christ,

Emily

Appendix 2

A HEDGE OF DOUBT

Lore Ferguson

Lore Ferguson is a writer at Sayable.net and has openly struggled with doubt and faith. She shares here one moment of reflection on doubt, God's gifts, and His protection.

I woke this morning for the first time in weeks without the heaviness of condemnation on me. I haven't been able to shake those feelings lately, no matter how hard I've pressed myself against the robe, no matter how much I've bent my face over Jesus' feet. I'll be honest: I've begun to doubt some things. Even now, writing this, my mind is replaying a litany of doubts. Do you really believe God loves you? Do you really believe you're worth something to Him? Do you really believe that anyone could love you at all? What makes you think He'll be happy with you?

They pile up and attack what I know to be true. And so this morning when I woke up gently, quietly, I held my breath for a moment or two, waiting for the doubts to assemble and charge. But they didn't. And I couldn't figure out why.

One of the greatest gifts God gave me was the gift of doubt. I doubt that many of us would see it as a gift, but I know it to be the deepest grace to me. He gave me the wide pasture of doubt and the pleasant boundary line of truth. He wounds me with my doubt but heals with me with His truth.

Like most who grew up in a church of one kind or another, I bought the lie that a fortified moralism would lead me to paths of great joy—purity until marriage, marriage by twenty-two, children by twenty-four, ducks lined up before me and behind me. I got them in a row. I organized my life to make sense.

And then life didn't make sense. Life dealt me, as one person called it, a bad hand. I'll never forget walking away from that conversation, wondering how to play those cards. What do you do with a handful of threes and no partner in this game? I'll tell you what you do: *you doubt.*

You fall full into it, bathe yourself in it, wash your soul with sin and shame. When the answers you've been given by well-meaning people fail, when the theology you believe (that God responds when we pray harder, give more, seek deeper, and repent faster) proves you the fool, and when God does not *seem* good, I'll tell you what you do: *you doubt.*

And here's the thing about doubt: it is a seemingly endless plateau. God has given us the gift of reason and logic and thought, so doubt will take us where nothing else can, because there is always another question, another possibility. Even if we bump up against a wall of truth, we are like little squares in Atari games, bouncing for eternity.

Doubt doesn't seem like a gift.

This morning I read the first chapter of Job, the righteous man who, we might also say, was dealt a bad hand. But today I noticed a word: *hedge*. "Have you not put a hedge around him . . . and all that he has?" (Job 1:10). The enemy asked God before he unleashed upon Job the full fury of his minions.

God permitted the enemy to do what he would, only that he must keep his hand from Job himself; and today I think about the hedge God has set around us. I want to believe that the hedge prevents the enemy from coming in, but that is not what we're told. No, the hedge prevents the enemy from going outside the bounds of what God has set for him. It is Job's hedge, but it is also the enemy's.

This morning I woke up and felt myself hit the hedge. Not my limitations, but God's. Not the end of myself, but the time when God holds up His hand and says, "No more. This is the safest place I have for you, within these boundary lines. Here. All the rest I have for you lies within these boundaries, and all the struggles I have for you lie within these boundaries. But do not worry: I have set this hedge around you, and the enemy will not prevail."

NOTES

Chapter 1: Fear of Man

1. Lou Priolo, *Pleasing People: How Not to Be an Approval Junkie* (Phillipsburg, NJ: P&R, 2007), 64.
2. Timothy Keller, *The Freedom of Self-Forgetfulness* (Chorley, UK: 10Publishing, 2013), Kindle edition, loc. 211–309.
3. I am drawing upon Keller, *The Freedom of Self-Forgetfulness*, Kindle edition, loc. 211–309.
4. Trillia Newbell, *United* (Chicago: Moody, 2014), 45.
5. Keller, *The Freedom of Self-Forgetfulness.*

Chapter 2: Fear of the Future

1. Thomas O. Chisholm, William M. Runyan, Sara Groves, "He's Always Been Faithful," from the album *Conversations* (Carol Stream, IL: Hope, 2001).

Chapter 3: Fear of Other Women

1. See Elyse Fitzpatrick, *Women Helping Women: A Biblical Guide to Major Issues Women Face* (Eugene, OR: Harvest, 1997).
2. *ESV Study Bible*, ed. Wayne Grudem (Wheaton, IL: Crossway, 2008), note on Romans 15:7.

Chapter 4: Fear of Tragedy

1. Sharon Begley, "Afraid to Fly after 9/11, Some Took a Bigger Risk—In Cars," March 23, 2014, *Wall Street Journal*, http://online.wsj.com/news/articles/SB107999266401462105.
2. "Though the word 'like' may indicate this is to be understood metaphorically, there are both ancient and modern accounts on record of people sweating blood—a condition known as hematidrosis, where extreme anguish or physical strain causes one's capillary blood

vessels to dilate and burst, mixing sweat and blood." *ESV Study Bible*, ed. Wayne Grudem (Wheaton, IL: Crossway, 2008), note on Luke 22:44.

3. Andreas J. Köstenberger and Justin Taylor, *The Final Days of Jesus: The Most Important Week of the Most Important Person Who Ever Lived* (Wheaton, IL: Crossway, 2014), 93.

Chapter 5: Fear of Not Measuring Up

1. Kevin DeYoung, *Crazy Busy: A (Mercifully) Short Book about a (Really) Big Problem* (Wheaton, IL: Crossway, 2014), 26.

Chapter 6: Fear of Physical Appearance

1. Trillia Newbell, "Mirror Wars," *Relevant*, April 17, 2013, http://www.relevantmagazine.com/life/whole-life/mirror-wars.

2. National Institute of Mental Health, "Statistics," http://www.nimh.nih.gov/health/publications/the-numbers-count-mental-disorders-in-America/index.shtml#Eating.

3. Emily Wierenga, "An Open Letter to My Friends Struggling with Eating Disorders," August 11, 2014, http://www.desiringgod.org/blog/posts/an-open-letter-to-my-friends-struggling-with-eating-disorders.

4. Milton Vincent, *A Gospel Primer for Christians: Learning to See the Glories of God's Love* (Bemidji, MN: Focus, 2008), 88.

Chapter 7: Fear of Sexual Intimacy

1. Morgan Bennett, "The New Narcotic," *The Public Discourse*, October 9, 2013, http://www.thepublicdiscourse.com/2013/10/10846/?utm_source=RTA+Bennet+Part+One&utm_campaign=winstorg&utm_medium=email.

2. Ibid.

3. Ibid.

4. Vickie Tiede, *When Your Husband Is Addicted to Pornography* (Greensboro, NC: New Growth Press, 2012), 22.

5. John Piper, "Hijacking Back Your Brain from Porn," *Desiring God*, October 9, 2013, http://www.desiringgod.org/blog/posts.

Chapter 8: Why We Can Trust God

1. *ESV Study Bible*, ed. Wayne Grudem (Wheaton, IL: Crossway, 2008), note on Proverbs 1:7.

2. J. I. Packer, *Knowing God* (Downers Grove, IL: InterVarsity, 1973), 23, emphasis original.

3. Ibid., emphasis original.

4. A. W. Tozer, *The Attributes of God: Deeper into the Father's Heart*, vol. 2 (Camp Hill, PA: Christian Publications), 144.

5. *Merriam-Webster Online*, s.v. "wisdom," http://www.merriam-webster.com/dictionary/wisdom.

6. "William Cowper," *Hymnary.org*, http://www.hymnary.org/person/Cowper_W.

7. William Cowper, "God Moves in a Mysterious Way," *Hymnary.org*, http://www.hymnary.org/text/god_moves_in_a_mysterious_way.

8. D. A. Carson, *The Difficult Doctrine of the Love of God* (Wheaton, IL: Crossway, 2000), 39.

9. *ESV Study Bible*, ed. Wayne Grudem (Wheaton, IL: Crossway, 2008), note on 1 John 4:8.

Chapter 9: The Fear of the Lord

1. Trillia Newbell, "The Feminine Focus," in *Good: The Joy of Christian Manhood and Womanhood*, eds. Jonathan Parnel and Owen Strachan (Minneapolis, MN: *Desiring God*, 2014), electronic book, 40–46.

Chapter 10: When Your Fears Come True

1. Trillia Newbell, "Creator, Redeemer, Friend," in *ESV Women's Devotional Bible*, © 2014 by Crossway, a publishing ministry of Good News Publishers. Used by permission. All rights reserved.

2. *ESV Study Bible*, ed. Wayne Grudem (Wheaton, IL: Crossway, 2008), note on Mark 4:37.

3. Wayfarer, "Jesus, Savior, Pilot Me," from the album *The River*, July 22, 2012, http://wayfarerseattle.bandcamp.com/track/jesus-savior-pilot-me.

Chapter 11: Growing in the Fear of the Lord

1. Edward Welch, *Running Scared: Fear, Worry, and the God of Rest* (Greensboro, NC: New Growth Press, 2007), Kindle edition, loc. 229.

2. Kevin DeYoung, *Taking God at His Word: Why the Bible Is Knowable, Necessary, and Enough, and What That Means for You and Me* (Wheaton, IL: Crossway, 2014), 18.

3. Ibid., 88.

4. The author of the hymn is unknown but is most likely Robert Keene. See http://www.challies.com/articles/hymn-stories-how-firm-a-foundation-free-download.

ACKNOWLEDGMENTS

How do you adequately thank all the people who have made something like this possible? You don't. I can't find the words to say, but I know my heart is full.

Thank you to Moody Publishers and their team for acquiring *Fear and Faith*: René Hanebutt, Holly Kisly, and Judy Dunagan. Thank you also to Janis Backing, who has helped get the word out about the book. I appreciate your efforts. Thank you also to my editor, Lydia Brownback.

Thank you to Wolgemuth and Associates for working with me throughout this process. Thanks specifically to Erik Wolgemuth, my agent. I am thankful to work with you and partner on this publishing journey. Writing *Fear and Faith* would have been a great challenge without your support and assistance.

I am thankful for friends who read my work and pray for me. Thank you, Kristie Anyabwile, Gloria Furman, Catherine Parks, and Amy Maples. I really love you, friends. Thank you also, Courtney Reissig, for praying and our many chats about writing and life. Thank you to all the amazing women who contributed their stories for *Fear and Faith*. I am confident the Lord will use them to bless and encourage those who read: Christina Fox, Gloria Furman, Eva Crawford, Nikki

Daniel, Lindsey Carlson, Jasmine Baucham, Megan Hill, Tara Barthel, Amy Maples, Donna Mitchell, Emily Wierenga, Christa Black, and Lore Ferguson.

Thank you to Susan Alexander, features editor at the *Knoxville News-Sentinel*, and to Christina Southern, dear friend and editor at KNS, for giving me my first stab at writing. Writing for the *Sentinel* was a blessing and joy. I learned so much from you and will always be grateful.

Thank you to the ERLC and CBMW. Your support over the year has been amazing. I am so honored to get to work with such wonderful organizations. But it's the people who make the organizations. I am grateful for you who labor alongside me and cheer me on in the Lord.

Thank you to the many readers who have written to let me know how my work has encouraged them. It keeps me going! Thank you for building my faith for writing. Your words are very meaningful.

Thank you to my family: Tennion, Barbara, and Momma Reed. I love you all so very much. Thank you also to my church family. Your prayers and support have been a blessing and great encouragement.

Thank you to my dearest friend and wonderful husband, Thern. There is absolutely no way I'd be able to do anything without your love, support, prayers, and kindness. I really can't believe how supportive and eager you are to see the Lord use my writing for His glory. I can't fully express my love and thankfulness to you, my friend and love. I love you! And thank you little babies, Weston and Sydney (you will always be my babies).

Thank You, Lord! I pray that You use this little book

for the good of those who read it, and I do pray it brings You glory, Lord. Thank You for the gift of faith, teaching me about You through Your Word and by Your Sprit, suffering the wrath that I deserve, and loving me. I know I love You because You first loved me.

rightnow MEDIA

FREE BIBLE STUDY VIDEOS FOR

FEAR
AND
FAITH

BECAUSE YOU HAVE PURCHASED
FEAR AND FAITH, YOU ALSO
HAVE FREE ACCESS TO THE COMPANION
BIBLE STUDY VIDEOS - PERFECT FOR
GROUP STUDY OR PERSONAL DEVOTION

TO ACCESS THESE VIDEOS FOR 90 DAYS,
VISIT RightNowMedia.org/FearandFaith
AND USE PROMO CODE: NoFear